Heritage of Tibet

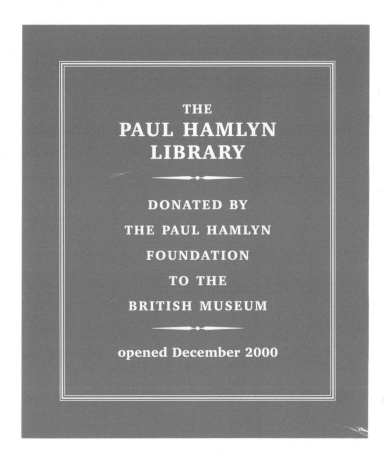
1 (overleaf) Scene outside the cathedral (Jo-khang) of Lhasa during the scapegoat ceremony.
(Photo H. E. Richardson)

W. Zwalf

Heritage of Tibet

PUBLISHED FOR THE TRUSTEES OF THE BRITISH MUSEUM
BY BRITISH MUSEUM PUBLICATIONS LIMITED

© 1981 The Trustees of the British Museum

Published by British Museum Publications Ltd,
46 Bloomsbury Street, London WC1B 3QQ

British Library Cataloguing in Publication Data

Zwalf, W.
  Heritage of Tibet.
  1. Tibet – Civilization
  I. Title
  951.5   DS786
  ISBN 0–7141–1420–0

Designed by Sebastian Carter

Set in Monophoto Plantin by
Northumberland Press Ltd, Gateshead, Tyne and Wear
and printed in Great Britain by
Fletcher and Son Ltd, Norwich

Contents

Acknowledgments

The author wishes to thank H. E. Richardson for generously answering many questions and giving permission to reproduce photographs; J. Lowry for much encouragement and advice; D. L. Snellgrove, P. Denwood and Lama Chime Radha for sparing time to answer questions; colleagues in the Department of Conservation in the British Museum for much patience and enthusiasm in giving technical information. The use made of the Newark Museum's *Catalogue of the Tibetan collection* is gratefully acknowledged.

2 Seated figure of an unidentified lama holding his hands in the gesture of instruction. Brass with silver inlays on the eyes and on the monastic jacket. Height 14 in. 15th century AD (?).

Introduction

Tibet is for many a land of fascination and mystery and its ancient culture rightly commands deep interest and respect. In itself the country may seem insignificant, thinly populated and in one of the most inhospitable regions of Asia between the great civilisations of India and China. Nevertheless, behind its mountain barriers Tibet evolved a unique form of government and a complex culture made up of many strains both native and foreign in which religion predominated. On the one hand, it maintained ancient indigenous beliefs in the magical and hostile power of the forces of nature; on the other, Tibet adopted with great fidelity, but not without its own dynamic, the highly developed Buddhism of India before its progressive disappearance from the land of its birth in the thirteenth century. This huge inheritance provided Tibet with philosophy, theology, intense meditative techniques and another tradition of magical practice. Together the inherited and imported elements made up an amalgam which gives the Buddhism of Tibet its distinctive character. It is often called – though not by Tibetans – Lamaism, after the name they give to the Buddhist teacher or *bla-ma* (pronounced 'lama'), a word translating the Sanskrit *guru*, for throughout Tibetan Buddhism runs a special veneration for the one that teaches: doctrine and scripture are valueless without their controlled transmission by one qualified to initiate and assess the psychology and aptitude of the student. At stake was not the mere acquisition of knowledge but the prospect of salvation by one or other of the methods the religion had evolved. It is little wonder that in time Tibet became a theocracy ruled by the monasteries in partnership with the nobility.

Whether worshipping and propitiating the fierce spirits of his environment or engaging in meditation and the study of subtle theologies in the monasteries, the Tibetan in more recent times pursued his religion and the way of life it had so influenced with little interference from the outside world until 1951. While the Chinese Empire, the official suzerain, had been at the mercy of western powers and India was part of the British Empire, the

9

Tibetan, conscious of threats to his culture and religion and fearing economic exploitation, had needed little persuasion to keep his country closed to the European foreigner in particular. Thus while the cultures of India and China were being widely explored by nineteenth-century Orientalism, scholarly knowledge of Tibet lagged behind. The intellectual and physical barriers had together the effect of investing Tibet with mystery and leaving too many aspects of Tibetan life and culture obscure.

This picture, however, requires some modification. Despite formidable physical barriers Tibet has been a closed country for only a short period in its history. Relations with India were intense for a long time, as the adoption of Buddhism shows; the Mongols several times played a decisive political role; Christian missions were active in the seventeenth and eighteenth centuries and China has been culturally and politically influential from the earliest times to the present day. Even during the closure of Tibet in the nineteenth and twentieth centuries, coinciding with the growing European study of Oriental cultures, there was a measure of contact through both China and British India. At first this interest, in keeping with the general direction of European Orientalism, was linguistic. In 1834 the first Tibetan grammar and dictionary were published; knowledge of the language, though on a modest scale, was maintained amongst French, Russian, American and British scholars and manuscripts and blockprinted texts entered foreign libraries. European explorers were even able to visit outlying parts of Tibet, while its home provinces remained obstinately closed, and British officials in India acquired the language on the Himalayan borderlands where Tibetan culture was, as it still is, living and accessible. Thus when the British Mission led by Francis Younghusband forced its way to Lhasa in 1904 there were not only fluent speakers of Tibetan amongst its officers, but thanks to the painstaking reports of Indian agents, the so-called Pundits, who were secretly sent to survey Tibet after 1866, there even existed already remarkably full and accurate accounts of its religion, customs and geography.

Since Tibetans were not prevented from entering British India and Chinese suzerainty ensured a measure of communication between central Tibet and Peking, Tibetan objects began to enter Western collections. Thus in 1893 the British Museum acquired a sizeable number of Lamaistic images from a collection formed in Peking and in the following years there were further significant accessions, particularly from the Tibetan fringes of India as well as from Sikkim and Bhutan. There are many distinguished public collections in Europe (Paris, Leyden, Rome, Leningrad), the United States (the Newark Museum has published an excellent catalogue) and in this country (Victoria and Albert Museum, London, and Merseyside Museums, Liverpool); there is also much important material in private hands. Notwithstanding this and the remarkable assemblage of objects brought together at the great Tibetan exhibition of 1977 in Paris and Munich, the arts and crafts, like other aspects of Tibetan culture, remain insufficiently studied and the chronology, localisation of styles and techniques continue to pose obstinate problems. The explorations of Giuseppe Tucci in central and western Tibet between 1927 and 1948 point to what might have been achieved by systematic documentation of buildings and their contents in the light of historical and iconographic documents. It is quite uncertain how far such investigations, if they could be conducted today, would contribute to a solution of these same problems.

The rapid secularisation of Tibet by the People's Republic of China since 1951 makes it likely that many of the observations lost to scholarship while Tibet was closed in the nineteenth and some of the twentieth centuries can never be made good. Tibetans in exile, however, are showing great concern with the preservation of their heritage and the cultural outposts south of the Himalayan border are being increasingly studied. There are indications, moreover, that the Chinese authorities may acknowledge the strength of Tibetan traditions more in the future and it is to be hoped that the tourism now being permitted will be followed sooner or later by fieldwork. It is too early, however, to judge how well the old and the new may become reconciled in Tibet itself.

This book is intended as an introduction to some of the objects in the British Museum's magnificent collections and the culture that created them. For discussions on many of the questions not dealt with here, the reader's attention is directed to the bibliography. One difficulty in discussing Tibet should be mentioned. It lies in the difficult and unfamiliar forms of written Tibetan. Since the general reader is not expected to be familiar with these forms, the Sanskrit terms of Buddhism, more easily pronounced at sight and more 'international', have been preferred everywhere to their Tibetan equivalents. Where no choice was possible the written rather than the spoken forms of Tibetan have normally been given, in accordance with a general and preferable practice; geographical names are, however, used in their more familiar forms.

Another difficulty is the term Tibet itself, which can be defined in two different ways, one political, the other ethnic and cultural. Political Tibet, since 1965 the Autonomous Region of Tibet within the People's Republic of China, covers some 500,000 square miles. Its capital is Lhasa and it contains the areas of settlement made possible by the great rivers in the west, south and east as well as considerable upland tracts, especially in the north-west. Much of this region was controlled by the Dalai Lama's government until 1951. Ethnic and cultural Tibet is a much larger area and more difficult to define. It includes territory where the Tibetan language or closely related forms are spoken and Tibetan religion was once practised. This area extends in the north and east into the Chinese provinces of Qinghai and Sichuan, where the frontier was formerly in dispute and control was erratically exercised from Lhasa or by China. Throughout this area there were monasteries loyal to the spiritual authority of Lhasa and here and there semi-independent princedoms. Beyond Qinghai on the north and separated by the Gansu corridor connecting China Proper with Xinjiang is Mongolia, a country with a different language and people but, between the seventeenth and twentieth centuries, to a great extent spiritually subject to Lamaism and using Tibetan as a language of Buddhist culture and prayer. On the south from Burma to Kashmir, where the political border joins India, Bhutan and Nepal, there are still populations speaking Tibetan and following one or other of the Lamaist sects. In varying degrees Bhutan and Sikkim (now within the Indian Union), parts of Nepal (Walung, Solu-Khumbu, Mustang, Dolpo and Mulu) and Zanskar, Spiti, Kulu, Lahul and Ladakh (sometimes called Indian Tibet) are all outposts of the old Tibetan culture. Unless the distinction is specifically made references to Tibet in this book will normally refer to the entire cultural area.

Map of the Tibetan Autonomous Region of the People's Republic of China. The shaded area indicates land above 10,000 feet. Certain frontiers are in dispute.

13

I
The Land and its People

Tibet, the world's highest country, falls into three great physical divisions. Most of the country lies well over 10,000 feet above sea-level and forms part of the mountainous Alpine Fold Belt running from Europe through the Middle East and Central Asia into China and the Pacific Ocean. It is bounded on the south by the Himalayan system of several parallel ranges, with peaks rising to over 20,000 feet – Mount Everest is almost 30,000 – and passes never lower than 15,000 feet. On the western frontier the Karakorums link the Himalayas with the Kunlun mountains which run north-west, delimiting Tibet until they curve south of the Tsaidam Basin, which is in the Chinese province of Qinghai. The first of the physical divisions includes Amdo, to the east of the Tsaidam Basin, and the great Koko Nor lake, 10,000 feet above sea-level and about 40 miles wide and 60 long. Around the lake lies excellent pasture and agricultural land and nearby were important monasteries. Much of the Tsaidam, however, is a marshy plain bounded on the north by the Nanshan mountains beyond which is the Gansu corridor linking China Proper with Xinjiang where ancient trade-routes ran to the west. Tibet lies relatively open and accessible on the north-east and the adjoining regions all had connections with Tibet at different times in its history; the link with Mongolia has been particularly close.

The eastern limits of Tibet, also part of the same division and running north–south across mountain ranges and river valleys, border the Chinese provinces of Gansu, Sichuan and Yunnan, to rejoin the Himalayan system north of Assam. In this Sino-Tibetan frontier area run the upper reaches of the great rivers of eastern Asia, the Huanghe or Yellow River, the Yangtse, the Salween and the Mekong, which flow along valleys running more or less north–south and reach the sea through China, Burma and Vietnam. These valleys are sometimes as low as 6,000 feet, well watered and very fertile, with forests and good grazing land. Rainfall, provided by the monsoons through Assam and Yunnan, is plentiful, in contrast to most of Tibet. This eastern part of the country, south of Amdo, is called Khams.

15

3 Nomad herdsman from grazing grounds south of Nam Tso Lake. (Photo H. E. Richardson)

The whole of Tibet is sometimes called a plateau, and this term is particularly appropriate of another of the great divisions, the Byang-thang, an area of plains and valleys with an average elevation of about 15,000 feet and peaks much higher. It extends more than 800 miles from east to west and contains numerous saline lakes with shores rich in potash, borax and soda deposits. It is an inhospitable land, where low rainfall and icy winds which blow throughout the year prevent the growth of trees and crops. Only a sparse covering of grasses affords poor grazing for the yaks and sheep of the nomad population.

The third division lies in the south, where the great rivers of the Indian subcontinent have their sources. The Indus and Sutlej rivers, rising in western Tibet, flow into Pakistan. India's sacred river, the Ganges, has its source just inside this part of Tibet. The Tsangpo, which rises in the same region, flows eastwards between the Himalayan and Transhimalayan ranges for some 800 miles, receiving a number of tributaries, before turning south into India, where it becomes the Brahmaputra and discharges into the Bay of Bengal. Towns, including the capital Lhasa, small settlements and great monasteries lie in the valleys of the Tsangpo system in central Tibet which also provide good grazing and agricultural land. The cultural and political centre of Tibet has always been here, in the provinces of dBus and gTsang.

One of Tibet's poetic names is 'Land of Snows'. In fact, precipitation, either rain or snow, is not high because the Himalayas close the central landmass to the water-bearing clouds from the sea areas. Rainfall is highest in the east and north-east and falls mainly between April and November. Most of Tibet receives between ten and twenty inches of rain a year; the perpetual snow-line is between 16,000 and 20,000 feet and reported falls of seasonal snow are of up to four feet and are slow to melt. The climate is dry and cold, with frost for about eight months, and the air can be very clear. Night and day temperatures differ spectacularly, sometimes varying by as much as 80–90°F, although the normal variation lies between 50° and 60°F. While Lhasa temperatures during the short summer can be as high as 90°F in the shade, the winter range in most of Tibet is between −20° and 40°F. One characteristic of the climate is the ferocity of the winds. Days can start bright and sunny until about midday, when gales develop and blow until sundown, or even continue through the night. These winds are particularly trouble-some when they carry dust and gravel. Caravans have to stop and horsemen are blown from their mounts. Hailstones, sometimes up to three inches in diameter, are a great hazard for crops, livestock, nomad tents and, indeed, human life. Against this multiple threat magicians were retained by both the government and individuals.

The habitable regions of Tibet fall into two broad economic divisions: pastoral and agricultural. Pasture is found mainly to the north wherever the

16

4 Herdsmen's tent at an encampment beyond Stag-lung, north of Lhasa. (Photo H. E. Richardson)

land is not too inhospitable; agriculture is practised in the southern and eastern valleys, where alluvial deposits have created arable soil and the valleys trap the sunshine. Even where rainfall is low, mountain streams and other water courses provide adequate supplies both for irrigation and for turning mills. Nevertheless, some rain in summer is necessary for the crops. The pastoral and agricultural ways of life are often mixed or follow the transitions of the terrain: above the cultivated southern valleys lie slopes suitable for grazing.

The economic balance of old Tibet depended largely on the inter-dependence of the two ways of life. In the vast grazing regions of the north lived nomads who kept herds of yak, sheep and goats and made their homes in yak-hair tents. The products of the herding economy were meat, butter, cheese and wool, which were traded for the artefacts and imports brought from the settled zone. In the valleys, between 8,000 and 12,000 feet above sea-level, where trees can grow, are the villages with their brick and stone

17

5 Wooden box for *rtsam-pa*, or roasted barley flour which is mixed with butter tea and made into small balls and eaten. Height 4½ in., diameter 9 in. 19th–20th century AD.

houses, as well as the few towns, the temples and monasteries. Amongst willow groves grow barley, oats, wheat, peas, beans, mustard, potatoes, radishes and turnips. In lower parts of the country peaches, apricots, pears and walnuts are found; to the east grapes are grown and, in the extreme south-east where the monsoon rains spill over into Tibet, rice and maize. Barley is particularly suited to Tibetan conditions for it will grow at heights of 15,000 feet or even higher. The flour when roasted, mixed with tea and butter and kneaded into a ball, is called *rtsam-pa* and is eaten in much of the country. The very dry climate enables cereals to be stored for up to fifty years and other foodstuffs and various substances will keep for long periods. It is reported that Tibetans would lay in their meat supply of yak's meat and mutton in October and hang it from a ceiling; nine months later it was still free from offensive smell. Mutton five years old was not unusual.

Despite the difficult terrain and the effect of the seasons on travel, Tibet was linked with her neighbours by a number of trade-routes, which carried exports of wool, furs of the fox, stone marten, lynx and marmot, yak-tails, hides, the soft under-wool of the shawl-wool goat, borax, salt, musk and

18

medicinal herbs as well as ponies and mules. The beasts of burden were mules, yaks, donkeys, sheep and goats, the latter mostly in western Tibet. Mules were reputed the best climbers but yaks could negotiate what seemed impossible rocks and boulders. Routes to India led westwards to Ladakh (Leh), Kashmir and Almora and southwards to Kalimpong, and at one time a route through Nepal was much used. From India Tibet imported cotton and woollen goods, hardware, corals, precious stones, tobacco, dried fruits, sugar, molasses, matches, needles and soap; from Bhutan and Nepal came rice, and Bhutan also supplied wood. The route to China ran through the ethnic border town Tatsienlu and carried Chinese brick tea, silks, satins, brocades, cotton goods and scarves in exchange for musk, gold-dust, wool, sheepskins, furs and medicinal herbs. To the north lay the road to Mongolia passing the great Koko Nor lake; caravans brought Chinese silver, silk and ponies in and took away woollen cloth, incense sticks and copies of Tibetan scriptures, for Mongolia, a Buddhist country, had been evangelised from Tibet. The northern route also brought pilgrims from the outlying inhabited parts of the north-east to the shrines and sanctuaries of the Tibetan heartlands. This arduous route was served by only two caravans a year. In addition to weather hazards was the constant danger from bandits. It was small wonder that in more recent times travellers from China preferred the sea-route and the short land journey from Calcutta to Lhasa.

On the Tsangpo river, navigable for some 400 miles, plied the Tibetan coracles of yak-hide stretched on a framework of thorn scrub or willow. They were capacious and often carried up to eight or nine people as well as beasts, goods and even heavy poplar and walnut logs. The boatman often kept on board a sheep to carry his supplies for the return journey which, since the eastward flow of the river was so strong, had to be made by land, while the coracle was carried by the boatman.

Writers generally agree that Tibetans are of mixed stock; some refer to them as Mongoloids and, while admitting admixture over the past, consider the Tibetans on the whole a fairly distinct type. There has been little investigation of anthropometric data (height, skull measurements, hair and eye colour) but these are said to vary considerably. Two major strains are distinguished: a round-headed type, predominant in the cultivated valleys, which may derive from the Yellow River basin and be related to the early Chinese and Burmese, while a long-headed type is found mainly among the nomads of the north, the Khams to the east, and the Lhasa aristocracy, who share with other noble families of central and western Tibet more or less legendary origins in the foreign populations of the north-east. The affinities of this second group seem to be with the Turkic peoples to the north. Other groups are recognised along the southern borders as of probably different origins again, such as the Mon, a name used to designate populations

7 Minister's summer hat with button of rank and pierced jade tube to hold a peacock's feather, awarded as an honour by the Chinese emperor. Rims of silk brocade with silver thread and red silk tassels over a plain cotton dome. Diameter 13 in. 19th century AD.

stretching from Ladakh in the west to the Sino-Tibetan border regions in the south-east.

The population of political Tibet seems to have fluctuated in recent times and estimates have varied. One puts the total number of inhabitants at about 1.5 millions before 1951 and 1.3 millions in 1971. A more recent figure is 1.7 millions. A decline in population was already commented upon by a British observer, Sir Charles Bell, in the earlier part of this century. Pointing to its effect on the agricultural workforce, he ascribed it to polyandry (the custom by which a woman was shared by a number of husbands, usually brothers), venereal disease and the drain into the monasteries and convents, where celibacy was the rule.

Two main divisions of the Tibetan population have already been mentioned, the valley farmers and the mountain herdsmen. The monks and nuns formed a sizeable proportion of the population, estimated at between a quarter and a sixth, and will be discussed in greater detail later. A nobility also existed and was made up of three groups by origin. The smallest group derived from the ancient kings who ruled Tibet between the seventh and ninth centuries; a larger number were a *noblesse de robe*, who had received titles and land in return for service in the administration and sometimes continued to hold official positions in the state for many generations; the

21

6 Two yak-hide coracles drawn up on the river bank. (Photo H. E. Richardson)

8 One of the two supervising nobles of the New Year games at Lhasa, wearing the permitted winter furs and his official ear-ring and flanked by attendants in ceremonial dress. (Photo H. E. Richardson)

third source was the families of Dalai Lamas who, even when of humble extraction, were automatically ennobled upon the recognition of the infant as the new Dalai Lama and received large estates. The nobility, who were addressed with special honorific forms of speech, shared in the administration with the priesthood and as landowners exercised considerable power over their tenantry. They drew their wealth from agricultural produce paid as dues in kind, from cash payments and their right to mounts and beasts of burden when required. From their herdsmen they also received appropriate dues of butter, cheese, yak-hair and yak-tails. Stewards administered this income and the houses of the nobility had store-rooms and stables in addition to the residential quarters. In summer they particularly enjoyed archery, using arrows with perforated heads which produced a whistling sound. As part of the entertainments connected with the New Year ceremonies, which they helped to supervise, nobles and officials supplied contingents of horsemen dressed in traditional armour in which they paraded; later their champions engaged in races and contests of archery and gunfire. Women of the nobility, dressed in their finest clothes, served beer to the aristocrats supervising the occasion.

Traders formed another section of the Tibetan population. They managed Tibet's imports and exports, travelling in caravans along the trade-routes. The basic needs of the Tibetan were met from within the country, with the exception of tea brought from China in the convenient form of bricks packed in yak-hide and carried by beasts of burden. Several kinds of Chinese tea were used; Indian tea never found a market in Tibet. Among foreign traders the Nepalese enjoyed a favoured status and they also supplied the country with craftsmen and artisans. The Tibetan trading class was, however, not very large. Tibetans were born traders and the three largest communities, the nomad herdsmen, peasants and monks, engaged in considerable trade between themselves. Thus salt and soda from the northern uplands were bartered for grain from the agricultural regions. The nobility had commercial agents who managed the produce of their estates and they also sent agents abroad to buy rare luxury items. The monasteries, particularly the larger, had their own administrative arrangements which involved the collection of rent in cash and kind from their estates and the storage and marketing of the produce. Monastic financial ventures included borrowing and lending money, conducting trading expeditions, the profits of which were sometimes used for the maintenance, repair, and expansion of the monasteries and for the provision of new images. Individual monks were also free to trade.

In certain towns were markets with their goods displayed beneath large umbrellas and awnings; offered for sale were tea, soda, salt, rugs, dyes, glue for paper-making, wooden cups for food and drink, salted river-fish which, like meat, kept well for many months in the Tibetan climate, vegetables, rice, grain, wool, dried and fresh fruit, jewellery and swords. There were also regular shops, often managed by women while their menfolk were away on trading journeys. In Lhasa were shops and a market near the cathedral (Jo-khang), larger shops consisting of basement rooms opening on to the street often with tables just outside. The better shops belonged to Ladakhis and Nepalis, while those open to the sky were kept by Tibetan women. Here the goods included the coarse woollen cloth made in most Tibetan households, squares of silk from China, cheap printed material from India, maize and rice from Bhutan, spices, the usual home-grown vegetables, tea-bricks, ritual objects, coral, amber and agate necklaces, talisman boxes and tea-cups of polished birch and maple. The stallkeeper was never without tea-pot of earthenware, cup and *rtsam-pa* bag.

The peasantry lived predominantly in the south and east in river valleys, on the lower slopes of the uplands and on fertile plateaux. The land they occupied belonged usually to a monastery or noble landowner whom they paid by various services, such as cultivation of other parts of the estate, working on roads, providing transport and digging and maintaining irrigation works. They harvested an annual crop from the best land and left poorer land fallow every second or third year. The harvest took place in September, and sowing a year or six months previously according to the quality of the land. Gathering in the crops could be a race with time against the winter frosts. For ploughing the farmer used the tractable *mdzo*, a cross-breed of bull and cow-yak; sowing and weeding were done by women. The yak and its cow, the *'bri-mo*, along with the cross-bred *mdzo* and *mdzo-mo,* the latter an unsurpassed milker, are characteristic animals of the Tibetan region. Other domesticated animals included common cattle, sheep, pigs, donkeys, mules, cats and chickens. A particular type of fierce black mastiff was used as a watchdog. The yak had numerous uses: it provided meat eaten fresh, frozen, cooked or raw; hair for tents, blankets, and strong ropes; hide for trunks, bags, boots and coracles; and fly-whisks were made from its tail. The yak can survive even the most difficult conditions; it finds its own food, and serves as a beast of burden. Mixed with tea, yak butter makes a particularly nourishing drink. The peasants cultivated barley, peas, wheat, oats, mustard, radishes and turnips. Mutton and yak beef were the commonest meat. The peasants built their houses of brick and stone to a height of up to two or three storeys, with verandahs fronting the upper windows. In the interior of the country the roofs were flat while sloping roofs are found in rainier areas on the southern Himalayan slopes or towards China. The commonest plan, also reflected in town houses, consisted of buildings around a central courtyard with the ground floor given over to animal shelter, forage and other storage. On the upper floors were the kitchen, bedrooms, the best room used as chapel and guest-room combined, and store-rooms. Access to these rooms was sometimes by wooden ladder or notched log which could be drawn up for defence. A farmer's furniture consisted of a few low tables, mattresses for sitting and sleeping and heavy wooden chests along the walls. Wooden pillars a few yards apart supported the roofs and ceilings. The flat roofs were used for stacking barley, drying grass for hay, storing firewood, burning incense and putting up prayer-flags.

A very different life was led by the herdsmen of the uplands who lived in

24

tents and moved according to the season and grazing conditions. In summer they pastured their herds on ever higher ground, staying as long as there was enough grass; in autumn they could often stay in one place as long as a month. Their herds consisted of yak and other cattle, ponies, sheep and goats and their diet was mainly cheese, curds and meat as well as the universal Tibetan butter tea. Vegetables and grains were not usual. Their black tent, unlike the round Mongolian tent, was four sided, with sloping roof, and usually had only one entrance. It could be thirty or more feet long and fifteen wide and was made of yak-hair woven into a coarse material. Near the entrance or in the centre was a fire-pit over which a stove was built to hold two or three large cooking pots, while a small hole in the roof allowed smoke to escape. The family's property and effects were stored along the walls of the tent in wooden chests and yak-skin bags. The kitchen equipment stood along one side of the tent and was sometimes screened off by a curtain. The nomads, like the peasants and townsfolk, had their domestic altar with images, butter lamps and offering bowls. At the end of the summer they would return to their permanent winter quarters where the tents were better protected: walls of yak dung were built near them as windbreaks and to help the dung dry before it was used as fuel. The winter encampment lasted for up to six or seven months, during which the herdsmen visited the towns and villages for supplies of tea, sugar, rice, grain, dried vegetables and fruit, and to sell or barter skins and furs, leather, yak-hair rope, wool, salt, soda and butter as well as some of their sheep and yak.

The nomad herdsmen had a tribal organisation and every tribe a fixed territory within which there were smaller units or groups of several families, camping separately but close by each other. Each camp had a headman who had mainly moral authority but also saw to the collection of taxes. The decision to move to another grazing area was taken collectively after discussion by the group of camps which then formed a caravan and moved off after an offering of *rtsam-pa* in the fire-pit. Although in summer their encampments were far from a monastery the nomads were by no means irreligious and if they could afford it paid a monastery so that a monk could come and live among them as priest and teacher. They were ardent pilgrims and gave such wealth as they could to the monasteries. Older men might give up their wandering life to become monks and spend the rest of their lives atoning for the slaughter of animals for food and clothing which, despite Buddhist ethic, was practised all over Tibet to sustain the population against the extreme climate.

LANGUAGE

The Tibetan language belongs to the Sino-Tibetan family, a large group including, as the name indicates, Chinese. Another member is Burmese, to which Tibetan is more closely related, so that the term Tibeto-Burman is also used to designate the various forms of the two languages. While it may not always have been so, Tibetan is now a language of the monosyllabic type, that is to say, the elements of vocabulary are of one syllable and longer words can be analysed into one-syllable components. In the systems of trans-literation a hyphen separates the syllabic elements, rendering an equivalent sign in the Tibetan script. It will be observed from Tibetan names and words quoted that Tibetan often exhibits ungainly clusters of consonants. Most of these consonants are not pronounced in the speech of Lhasa and central Tibet or in the widespread and very similar standard pronunciation of the sacred texts. The pronunciation of dialects on the edge of the Tibetan speech-area comes closer to such spellings and it may be assumed that the written language is based on an older Tibetan dialect which may not have been the predecessor of the central speech forms. Tradition has it that the first king to favour Buddhism, Srong-brtsan-sgam-po (c. AD 627–650), sent one of his ministers, Thon-mi Sambhota, to Kashmir in AD 632 and that this minister brought back an Indian script which he adapted to the needs of Tibetan. The modern printed character differs very little from it (9). The derivation of Tibetan writing from Indian scripts of the seventh century is clear enough; the only uncertainty lies in exactly determining the prototype; some scholars accept that it may have been one used in the north-west.

The cultural importance of the Tibetan language and its written form lies in the role they played in the diffusion of Buddhism in Central Asia and the maintenance of the scholastic system that went with it. The great body of Buddhist literature in the Indian classical language, Sanskrit, which has no affinity with Tibetan, was translated into Tibetan so that by the end of the thirteenth century Tibetan Buddhists had ceased to be directly dependent on Indian religious authority. An unbroken succession from the original Indian masters to Tibetan pupils was reinforced by the availability to the Tibetan in his own language of texts, some of which no longer exist in the original (unless, indeed, they are rediscovered amongst the ancient books preserved in some of the older monasteries; their libraries have never been adequately explored). The completion of the vast work of translation coincided more or less with the destruction by Muslim conquerors of the great monasteries of Bihar and Bengal with their libraries (c. 1200). The translators had devised lists of equivalents for Sanskrit theological, ritual and philosophical terms so that uniformity in translating could be main-tained. This was done so successfully that lost Sanskrit originals can be

9 Lower part of an inscribed pillar about 7 ft high in the courtyard of bSam-yas monastery dating from the reign of Khri-srong-lde-brtsan (755–797) promising perpetual royal protection for the observance of Buddhism and confirming the privileges and property of the foundation. (Photo H. E. Richardson)

convincingly reconstructed from their Tibetan versions. This standardisation was extended to all texts already translated so that the Tibetan Buddhist has to this day a coherent vocabulary and phraseology with which to handle the sophisticated theological traditions that his ancestors adopted from many centuries of previous development in Indian Buddhism.

27

10 General view of the monastery of bSam-yas, the first Tibetan monastery, founded *c.* AD 779 in the reign of Khri-srong-lde-brtsan. (Photo H. E. Richardson)

2
History

The early history of Tibet is obscure and there is little certain information about the period preceding the united monarchy which, during the seventh century, enters Asian politics as an organised and aggressive state with a feudal structure based on the tenure of land by nobles and petty kings subordinate to the imperial centre. Most of what is reported about Tibet before this time is legend. There has been no archaeological work in Tibet, for the act of digging in the cause of historical enquiry and thus disturbing the earth would, according to the notions prevalent until recently, have been thought as unacceptable a desecration as mining. The Tibetan believed that the soil was inhabited by spirit beings who, even before ploughing and building, must be placated; excavation and mining were unforgiveable theft as well as disturbance. It is, however, in connection with the panning of gold that what may be the earliest references to Tibet, or its western borderlands, occur. An anecdote first reported by Herodotus (484–424 BC) and repeated in different form by other writers in antiquity tells how the vast quantities of gold which the Indians paid as tribute to their Persian overlords came from a desert (or the upper Indus) where the abundant gold-dust was gathered by giant ants with skins like panthers. The story has been explained as referring to the collection of gold by human prospectors from river valleys of western Tibet, where the fauna included panthers, which were a hazard, and large ants which impressed themselves on the minds of the gold-gatherers and grew in the telling of their adventures. The idea of ant-gold may have been widespread, for an ancient Indian word for gold is derived from that of the ant and even in recent times gold-digging ants occur in the folklore of western Tibet. Another reference from western sources is tantalisingly short. Amongst the Asian peoples north of India, the geographer and astronomer Ptolemy (second century AD) tells us, were the Bautai. The name seems to be related to the Tibetans' term for themselves and their country, which is written *Bod* in the archaic spelling of the language but now pronounced 'Pö'. Its earlier pronunciation as the Indians recorded it is reflected in the Sanskrit *Bhota*, and the name of the modern state of Bhutan is related to the same word. The name *Bod* has been explained as an old word meaning 'the native or original place'. 'Tibet' on the other hand seems to derive from the name of a people living in the north-east of the ethnic Tibetan region who figure as the 'Tupput' in Central Asian texts, the accounts of Muslim writers and early European authors on Asia. Marco Polo talks of the province of Thebeth but probably means a region nearer to China than the area around Lhasa. An etymology formerly offered for Tibet combines the word *Bod* with an adjective *stod*, now pronounced 'tö', meaning 'high' and so giving something like 'Upper Tibet'. Various other explanations for the word *Bod* are found in Tibetan writings.

The Tibetan legends attribute their own origins to the union of a monkey and an ogress whose descendants gradually acquired the basic human skills and with them human appearance. Descent from monkeys was also related of the Qiang, a warlike nomad people referred to by the Chinese as early as 1400 BC and inhabiting their north-western and western borders; according to the Chinese, the Tufan, as they called the Tibetans of the country unified in the seventh century, were a branch of the Qiang. While early traditions place Tibetan origins and legends variously on the eastern side of the country, the first clearly historical unit is found in the Yarlung Valley, a tributary entering the Tsangpo from the south in central Tibet. In this favourable setting the work of unifying the existing small states into a feudal empire was begun by conquest and marriage around AD 600. The first of the great kings, Srong-brtsan-sgam-po (*c.* AD 627–650), carried his conquests to the borders of China Proper, into Xinjiang, then a region of cosmopolitan culture and mainly Buddhist, and western Tibet, forming alliances by marriage with the Chinese Empire and Nepal. Tradition has it that Buddhism and the Tibetan script were introduced in his reign. Tibetan conquests continued after his death, principally in Xinjiang, where for some time the Tibetans controlled the ancient Silk Road, the route between China and the West, and left considerable quantities of literary remains, particularly in a walled-up store-room at Dunhuang on the edge of China itself; the Tibetans also thrust southwards, briefly, into India more than once and controlled territory south of the Hindu Kush passes (Gilgit). During the second half of the eighth century, in the reign of king Khri-srong-lde-brtsan (755–797), Tibetan power was at its height; the Chinese capital was taken and even in 822, when the country had weakened as a result of conflicts between the central authority, which adopted Buddhism as the state religion (779), and the feudal nobility allied with the native religion, a treaty recorded on a stone pillar still standing in Lhasa, recognised China and Tibet as equals. But when king Glang-dar-ma (838–842) was assassinated by a Buddhist monk for his anti-Buddhist policies the centralised monarchy fell apart into an age of feudal disintegration; the Central Asian empire was soon lost and the centre of culture, and a measure of stability, shifted to states in western Tibet where descendants of the old royal line ruled. Here the stage was set for the re-establishment and growth of Buddhism as a political power in Tibet. Monks from eastern Tibet are said to have restored the religion in Lhasa at the end of the tenth century, but it was the patronage of the western kingdom of Gu-ge with its capital at Tsaparang that gave the most powerful impetus to what is called the Second Diffusion of the religion, which from then onward became centred in the monasteries, the larger of which, well endowed and populous, began to play the part of landowner and noble in the political and economic structure of a fragmented and decentralised country.

Of the several sects that grew up during the Second Diffusion that of the Sa-skya-pa was the first to hold sway over most of the country. Their earliest monastery, which became a great landowner, was founded in 1073 at a site advantageously placed on a trade-route between the Nepal Valley and the agricultural area of Shigatse, and on the edge of a pastoral region where butter and wool were abundantly available. The spectacular rise of the Mongols as a great empire under Genghiz Khan led the Sa-skya abbot and two nephews to make submission on the country's behalf to Genghiz Khan's successor, Godan, in 1244. The Sa-skya abbot became Regent of Tibet for the Mongols in 1247; the Sa-skya power was strengthened when one of the nephews, 'Phags-pa, gained a religious influence over Khublai Khan, then (1253) still governor of a border region but soon to become Emperor of China (1260–94) and founder of its Mongol Yuan dynasty. Their relationship was described as 'Patron and Priest' (*Yon-mChod*): the religious ruler of Tibet acted as chaplain and mentor to the Emperor in return for his protection. An analogy has been drawn with the relationship between Pope and Holy Roman Emperor in the European Middle Ages. Although until 1358 a Sa-skya lama formally ruled a Tibet reorganised administratively under Mongol overlordship, there was much disunity within the country. The Sa-skya and their followers contended with the 'Bri-khung sect until the Sa-skya were victorious in 1290; on both sides men of religion behaved more like secular warriors and politicians. The Sa-skya soon lost their supremacy, however: the Mongols, expelled from China in 1386, were already too weak to interfere when in 1338 a member of the lay nobility, Byang-chub rGyal-mtshan of the Phag-mo-gru family, began, from a base in the Tsangpo Valley seventy-five miles from Lhasa, a career which led to his mastery of Tibet by 1350. He revived a sense of national identity, emphasising the unforgotten ancient monarchic ideal in alliance with the bKa'-rgyud-pa school, whose first great monastery had been founded by a member of his family. Nevertheless, the Mongol administrative reforms were retained and a connection with the Mongols after their expulsion from

China was continued. By their close connection with a monastic school, the bKa'-rgyud-pa, the Phag-mo-gru may be said to have continued religious rule. They were succeeded by secular regimes: in 1481 the princes of Rin-spungs became dominant in central Tibet and were followed from 1566 by a line of rulers of gTsang. Yet even these lines had the backing of another sect, that of the Karma-pa.

The seventeenth century saw the introduction of Dalai Lama government by a system depending on spiritual lineage through reincarnation. This system will be discussed in greater detail later (pp. 65ff). Its appearance coincided with renewed Mongol influence and the rise of the dGe-lugs-pa or Yellow Hat sect. Although their beginnings lay in the career of the reformer Tson-kha-pa (1357–1419) it was in 1578 that the abbot the dGe-lugs-pa monastery 'Bras-spungs (Drepung), bSod-nams rGya-mtsho, converted the chief of the Tumed, one of the Mongol tribes, and acquired for the Yellow Hats a powerful secular ally at a time when in Tibet itself they were in conflict with the Karma-pa, a sect which enjoyed the protection of the princes of gTsang. The chief of the Tumed Mongols, Altan Khan, conferred on bSod-nams rGya-mtsho the Mongolian title of Tale or Dalai, meaning 'ocean', a term expressive of spiritual eminence, and it was subsequently applied retrospectively to his two predecessors in the dGe-lugs-pa tradition. The Mongols' interest in Tibet and their protection of the dGe-lugs-pa was reinforced by the discovery of the fourth Dalai Lama reincarnation in the great-grandson of Altan Khan; another Mongol chief, Gushri Khan of the Qosot tribe, allied himself with the fifth Dalai Lama (1617–82) on whose behalf he intervened in Tibetan affairs in 1642, defeating the Prince of gTsang and his Karma-pa allies, and establishing himself as King of Tibet with the Dalai Lama as its religious leader. In this way the Patron–Priest relationship of earlier Mongol days was re-established and with it, as before under the Yuan dynasty, a high measure of secular authority for the priest. Under the fifth Dalai Lama the dGe-lugs-pa became the dominant school and remained so until 1959; monasteries belonging to other sects were taken over or reorganised and new monasteries were built. The well-known Potala at Lhasa, the imposing palace-monastery of the Dalai Lamas, dominating the capital from its hill some three hundred feet above the level of the town, was constructed in its present form under the fifth Dalai Lama. He encouraged scholarship and good religious conduct and his statecraft was such that regents, the secular authority representing the Mongol king, became completely subservient to him, especially after the death of Gushri Khan in 1655.

The death of the 'Great Fifth', as he came to be called, led to renewed troubles in Tibet and the growth of Chinese influence. China has always been vulnerable to invasion on its northern border as the Great Wall, built at the end of the third century BC, testifies and from 1644 a foreign dynasty, that of the Manchus, sat on the Imperial throne. Well informed on Central Asian matters and fearful that the Dzungar Mongols might become a threat to their Chinese empire, they encouraged the Qosot Mongol king Lhabzang Khan, descendant of Gushri, to install himself in Lhasa and kill the Regent, who had friendly relations with the Dzungars. Lhabzang Khan also removed the sixth Dalai Lama, a poet and libertine much loved by the Tibetans, but unsuited in the strict sense to the dignity he held. He was taken to eastern Tibet where he died. Lhabzang then installed a substitute – thought to be his natural son and also acceptable to the Chinese. Lhabzang Khan now paid tribute to the Chinese emperor, thus acknowledging himself as vassal (1706). Chinese power was soon actively involved, for the Dzungars, invited by disaffected monasteries, invaded Tibet in 1717, killed Lhabzang Khan and deposed his Dalai Lama, but they failed to bring with them the infant in whom many Tibetans saw the true incarnation of the original sixth. A Chinese army sent to expel the Dzungars brought with them the acceptable incarnation who was rapturously acclaimed; in the face of Tibetan resistance the Dzungars had already begun to withdraw. Under the Kangxi emperor (1662–1722) the Chinese proclaimed themselves as over-lords of Tibet and, to the satisfaction of the people, established the Dalai Lama they had brought with them as the true seventh (1720). Soon after, renewed internal strife led the Chinese to quarter a garrison in Lhasa with two civil officers called *Ambans*. In the peace that followed Tibet was effectively ruled for some twenty years by a wise and capable minister called Pho-la-nas. During some of this time the Dalai Lama was a minor and even as an adult remained under Pho-la-nas's influence. On his death Pho-la-nas's son attempted to expel the *Ambans* and the Chinese garrison; after a period of disorder a Chinese force arrived and with their support the Dalai Lama took control. The government was reorganised and the Dalai Lama con-firmed in his power with a council of four ministers, one of whom would be a monk. This reform of 1751 ended secular rule in Tibet: Pho-la-nas and his son, who had held the title of king, were the last lay rulers. From then on the government of the Dalai Lama and his religious assistants was never challenged; the nobility became subordinate as administrators and advisors of the religious ruler. Power was not, however, usually exercised by the Dalai Lama. During the period between the death of the seventh Dalai Lama (1757) and the assumption of power by the thirteenth (1895) Tibet was governed almost entirely by monks as regents, substitutes no longer for an absent or immature king, but practical necessities for a regime where succession by reincarnation rather than heredity made minorities inevitable. The reincarnated Dalai Lamas were recognised in childhood and the regents governing until they came of age were reluctant to lose their power.

Though no crime is proven, it is remarkable that after the death of the seventh Dalai Lama at the age of forty-seven none of his four successors lived beyond the age of twenty-one.

During this period there was Chinese intervention to repel invasion from Nepal, which in 1769 had become a Gurkha kingdom. A highly efficient expedition drove back the Gurkhas in 1792 and a reorganisation of the Tibetan government gave the *Ambans* an even greater power. Taxation was regulated, the system of finding the new Dalai Lama was – on paper – changed to a form of lottery and the relations of Tibet with foreign countries controlled by the simple means of closing the frontiers. This was intended to protect Chinese overlordship. The Tibetans were led to believe that the country and their religion would be endangered if foreigners were allowed into Tibet. With the Nepalese invasion fresh in their minds the Tibetans were induced to suspect that the growing British power in India had in some way been involved. With the closing of Tibet at the end of the eighteenth century it became for a little over a hundred years a forbidden land.

Throughout the nineteenth century British power in India established itself directly and indirectly on the borders of Tibet. Some of the territory incorporated into British India was Tibetan in culture. There was direct rule in Kumaon, Garhwal, Spiti, Lahul, Darjeeling and Kalimpong, and agreements with chiefs along the little-known border with north Assam. Nepal, Bhutan and Sikkim fell within the British sphere of influence. Contact with Tibet was confined to unofficial intermediaries and some of the country was explored by the so-called Pundits, specially trained Indians speaking Tibetan, who travelled through the country, often at some risk, observing manners, map-making and noting the system of government. Though enfeebled by internal decay China was still treated as the sovereign power. A British attempt to explore Tibet later in the century, though approved by the Chinese, was opposed by the Tibetans who invaded Sikkim in 1886 to prevent the departure of the expedition. Instead of an expedition there was a brief military engagement in which the Tibetans were forced back. Chinese agreement to the establishment of trade relations (1893) was again aborted by Tibetan intransigence, which, with increasing belief in Russian influence on the actually ruling thirteenth Dalai Lama, induced the Viceroy of India, Lord Curzon, to send an armed mission into Tibet. This, the well-known Younghusband expedition, reached Lhasa in 1904, not without resistance from the ineffective Tibetan army. In the absence of the Dalai Lama, who had fled to Mongolia, a treaty was signed with his government which settled outstanding questions without reference to the Chinese, a result overturned by an agreement two years later between Britain and China recognising Chinese suzerainty. A Chinese invasion followed and the Dalai Lama took refuge in India (1910). The fall of the

11 The Dalai Lama's tent for his arrival in Lhasa in 1939. This is a characteristic Tibetan tent with appliqué decoration which comprises a wheel motif surrounded by scrolling.
(Photo H. E. Richardson)

Manchu dynasty in 1911 and the subsequent weakness of the Republic effectively secured Tibet an independence maintained until 1951. During the Second World War Tibet expressed this by a strict neutrality and refusing consent to the construction of a supply road between China and India. Nevertheless, both before and after the War, the Chinese Republic attempted to establish its influence and both the Nationalist and Communists were agreed in claiming sovereignty over Tibet. After the Communist victory in China in 1949 the new People's Republic established an increasing degree of control over the country: between 1951 and 1959 alongside the diminishing authority of the Dalai Lama's institutions; after the Dalai Lama's flight to India in 1959 by an altogether more thorough policy of secularisation in which both the monasteries and the lay nobility, hitherto the twin supports of the theocracy, lost all their former jurisdiction. In 1965 Tibet was formally incorporated into the People's Republic as an Autonomous Region.

3
Religion

Tibet is probably best known as a stronghold of Buddhism, supposedly preserving a fossilised form of that religion after it had disappeared from its last
Indian centres in Kashmir, Bihar and Bengal. It is true that the student of
Indian Buddhism, particularly its later developments, is often led to supple-
ment his researches by learning Tibetan and a reason for this has been given
above in the brief description of the Tibetan language (pp. 26f). In Tibet
religion is, however, a much more complex phenomenon. The Buddhism
brought from India remained far from static; it interacted with native
religious beliefs, taking extensively from the folk religion, as well as from
a more specialised form of it called Bon, which is claimed as the earlier
or original religion of Tibet. In time, Bon, which has survived, like the
folk religion, into the present day, itself borrowed so largely from Buddhism
in a spirit of obvious competition as to seem in some ways its mirror image.
Knowledge of Bon is far less developed than that of Buddhism but with
the progress of Tibetan studies greater justice is being done to what has
been a neglected subject.

Writers on Tibetan religion have therefore referred in the plural to the
religions of Tibet, meaning the folk religion, called the 'religion of men', Bon
and Buddhism, the two latter organised into systems governed by the
monastery, ritual and scripture. Although Bon and Buddhism have been in
conflict, the organisation and beliefs of what has been called systematised
Bon are clear evidence of Buddhist influence and one of the Buddhist sects,
that of the rNying-ma-pa, which may conveniently be described as an
unreformed school of old believers, has significant features in common with
Bon. The folk religion has remained a powerful popular force accepted by
Buddhism, and its numerous local and nature gods are everywhere worshipped. Many cult acts of the Buddhist layman are those of the folk religion and
the large number of protector gods, well known in Buddhism but also
present among the Bon, are ancient nature spirits and demons. Overcome
and tamed, as the higher religions would claim, by their apostles and holy

37

12 A scene outside the cathedral (Jo-khan) at Lhasa during the scapegoat ceremony. Masked monks
wearing brocades represent protectors chasing away the scapegoats and the evil with them.
(Photo H. E. Richardson)

men, the protectors were bound by oath to use their often terrifying powers to defend the higher religions and their establishments. The great religious complexity and variety of Tibet is due to mutual influences at all levels over more than a thousand years and it is perhaps legitimate to think rather of one national Tibetan religion with many aspects.

The folk religion divides the world into three: heaven, atmosphere and earth, and peoples it accordingly with upper, middle and lower gods. The latter comprise water deities, often thought of as snakes, spirits of rocks and trees and earth gods who must be propitiated when the soil is tilled. Like the middle spirits of the air, thought of as red, savage and armoured huntsmen, they all, when offended, cause sickness and death. There are many legends connected with the mountain gods who belong to the middle region or atmosphere. There was also an ancient god of heaven surrounded by attendants, some of whom have, among the Buddhists, become demons. Other spirits included a field god, a tent god, a house god and a hearth god.

In a universe crowded with harmful demons the Tibetan naturally lived in a state of fear and frequently resorted to magic and exorcism. The services of the higher religions were not neglected but the remedies used went beyond reading scripture, building or repairing shrines and dedicating images. Exorcists performed various ceremonies and offerings included forms of ransom, which ranged from scapegoats, for instance two servants who were made to take upon themselves the sins of Lhasa, to the use of strips of wood on which was painted the figure of a man or woman according to the sex of the afflicted person (13). Evil spirits were also expelled by attacking them with charmed seeds thrown from horns carved with various devices which sometimes included the *phurb-bu* dagger (14). This implement consisted of a triangular iron blade and a handle which could take a number of forms. It was used not only to subdue evil spirits but also to conquer enemies and control the weather: it was thought capable of pinning an enemy to the ground and of flying great distances. Though no doubt rooted in ancient belief, this implement became linked with the higher religion and was thought to embody gods of the Buddhist school most closely connected with ancient Tibetan religion. Various ceremonies and beliefs were also connected with death. Some were accepted into the higher religion such as the *bar-do* (see p. 102) but others remained on a popular level, such as the means employed to banish ghosts, which were always thought malevolent. In a fire sacrifice for which dough effigies were stamped, using long pieces of wood carved with a variety of symbols and human and animal figures, the written name of the deceased was burnt. It is probable that this rite superseded an ancient sacrifice of living creatures. Another ancient element in Tibetan religion is divination and recourse to the oracle: old gods that had become protectors of Buddhism descended into mediums who provided

13 (left) Wooden ransom strip used in ceremonies to avert or remove affliction caused by hostile forces. The person to be ransomed is represented on the strip. The beneficiary here is wearing a fringed hat and the official's ear-ring. Length 7½ in. 19th–20th century AD.

14 (right) Metal *phur-pa* or *phur-bu*, a dagger for exorcism. A triple blade emerges from the head of a sea-monster. The fierce head beneath the *vajra* finial may be a form of Padmasambhava. Length 15¼ in. 19th century AD.

answers while in a state of trance. Even in the most recent times the government of the Dalai Lama used a State Oracle attached to the shrine at sNas-chung, west of Lhasa.

Bon, once a form of the ancient folk religion, has come to resemble Buddhism in many respects. During the early introduction of Buddhism into Tibet (seventh to ninth centuries AD) it served as a focus for feudal opposition to the central monarchy which patronised Buddhism. Bon is said

39

to have developed mainly in western Tibet, perhaps under Iranian and Hindu influences, and its early traditions and scriptures may have been recorded in a local language related to Tibetan. As with Buddhism its scriptures were then translated into Tibetan and its doctrines spread by missionaries. Bon claims a probably quite mythical founder in gShen-rab mi-bo whose legendary career shows close resemblances with the developed Buddha legend. This is the systematised Bon; in addition to its founder, it worships a god of wisdom, gShen-lha 'od-dkar and a reigning world god, Sangs-po 'bum-khri. The primordial principle is regarded as sometimes male and sometimes female. Gradually, Bon lost ground; the triumph of the Yellow Church in the seventeenth century was followed by persecution. Bon-po monasteries survived mainly in eastern and northern Tibet and in some other relatively inaccessible places. Bon images and paintings as the products of the same general culture resemble Buddhist art but there are differences, still insufficiently studied. There is only one Bon image in the British Museum (15).

15 Seated figure of a Bon deity, perhaps the god of wisdom, gShen-lha 'od-dkar, showing on his breast the Bon sacred letter 'a', representing pure sound. The swastika below the lotus beside his right shoulder is another Bon symbol. Height 5¾ in. 18th century AD (?).

BUDDHISM

The dominant religion of Tibet was a developed form of Buddhism which shows many differences from its earlier doctrines and from forms of the religion still practised elsewhere. Given the long history and wide diffusion of Buddhism, as well as the isolation of Tibet from the Buddhist world, this could hardly be otherwise. The religion was traditionally founded around 520 BC by one Siddhartha of the Gautama clan, known as Buddha or 'enlightened one'. Although he is conveniently referred to as the historical Buddha, his career as told in the scriptures became invested with legend and miracle and he must soon have been regarded as superhuman. For some forty years the Buddha wandered through parts of eastern India preaching his doctrine, ordaining monks and prescribing their disciplinary code and organisation. Buddhism has remained a monastic religion, nowhere more so than in Tibet, and monasteries have played a vital part in teaching and developing religious beliefs and their philosophical basis, even when the original impulsion came from outside their walls.

Early Buddhism accepted from the general religious environment of India the belief in reincarnation or the passage from life to life of the moral effect of actions: as a man sowed in one so he reaped in another. (The Buddha himself passed through many lives before his Enlightenment.) This proposition was linked in Buddhism with the concept that suffering was inseparable from life. Good actions led to good rebirths but their effect was temporary. Pain and sorrow were earned in retribution and would return when the good effects of previous actions had expired. Salvation could come only from the knowledge and practice summarised in the Four Noble Truths: the truth of suffering, for instance pain, loss and death; the truth of the cause of suffering, namely the ignorance that leads to desire for life and its false and temporary gratifications, for these are the motive-power of its renewal in sorrow; the truth of the cessation of suffering, the possibility of salvation from the series of rebirths through the destruction of ignorance and desire; and the truth of the means, the Noble Eightfold Path, a set of moral and meditational practices by which false views and retribution-earning acts were eliminated. The successful following of the Eightfold Path led to *nirvana,* the 'snuffing out' of the force that led to rebirth. A person who achieved this was an *arhat* and his physical death was his last. This became the early Buddhist ideal.

The Buddha died about 483 BC and his religion became an international faith, with all that this implied for the development of doctrine and practice, after its adoption by the Indian emperor Asoka (273–232 BC), who may have seen in it a binding agent for an empire with a mixed population, which even included Greeks on its north-western border. His patronage probably

41

16 Seated and painted wooden figure of the Buddha. Height 6½ in. Perhaps from south Tibet, 16th–17th century AD.

reflects the expansion of Buddhism into a widespread popular religion offering pilgrimage centres and a relationship of the monastery with layfolk which, in a highly developed form, was characteristic of Tibet centuries later. The monasteries provided spiritual guidance and pastoral activity and housed the shrines for the images of the Buddha and divine bodhisattvas created towards the end of the first millennium BC.

The creation of Buddhist images meant worship and the deification of the figures worshipped. The earthly teacher Siddhartha is unlikely to have been regarded as an ordinary man even in his lifetime. As Buddhism developed the historical Buddha was seen as an earthly form only of a heavenly Buddha who continued as the source of doctrine, expounding the subsequent teachings of the religion in celestial gatherings, just as his historical manifestation had taught monks and other hearers. These heavenly audiences included bodhisattvas, beings who had taken the vow, as had the historical Buddha in a distant and earlier life, to strive for buddhahood. The

17 Gilt brass Avalokitesvara with eleven heads and eight arms. The heads are explained as replacements for the god's original head which had burst with compassion. Height 13 in. China (?), 18th–19th century AD.

43

pattern of their striving was the career of the historical Buddha as a bodhisattva in his numerous previous lives: in each was performed some act of pre-eminent charity and self-sacrifice by which merit was accumulated and the entitlement to full Enlightenment was brought nearer. This process became the model for the follower of the developed religion but with this difference from the founder's life: now that the Doctrine had been proclaimed and established the need for Buddhas as initiators was replaced by another function. The bodhisattva who had advanced sufficiently to be entitled to buddhahood and *nirvana* renounced it and continued in the world as an active saviour until all beings had been brought to the same spiritual level. The early Buddhist gods were thought of as bodhisattvas, worshipped in image and deemed to be possessed of powers to save and assist which were inseparable from high spiritual achievement, and their number gradually increased. They bore names and were recognisable by specific attributes and postures. Prominent among them was Avalokitesvara, later the patron deity of Tibet. This development substituted for *nirvana* the lofty aim of saving oneself only so far as was necessary to save others. The earlier ideal of the *arhat* was considered selfish and its aim and practices suited to less evolved spirits. To the older Lesser Vehicle (*hinayana*) had been added the Greater Vehicle (*mahayana*) to salvation. This change took place in the first half of the first millennium AD. Alongside the development in cult and practice ran a current of philosophical enquiry and innovation. Indian philosophy, even before the historical Buddha's lifetime, had been concerned with the identification of the part with the whole: it sought unity in a single principle behind appearances. This now affected Buddhism. Early Buddhism had distinguished between the changing world of appearances, or *samsara*, and *nirvana*, which was a complete severance from it; there was ignorance and suffering and, opposed to it, liberation. In the philosophically more developed Buddhism the unifying principle was defined in two ways.

The Absolute, which had to be attained for salvation, was variously called 'emptiness', 'void', or 'suchness'; in it *nirvana* and *samsara* were shown to be essentially the same. One view held, somewhat negatively, that nothing definite could be said of either; another view held that appearances were false thought defiling pure consciousness. Since the Absolute lay beyond rational apprehension, techniques of mystical projections or constructions characterising the last stage of Indian Buddhism and its successor in Tibet were developed. The world of experience remained provisionally valid for the ordinary man and the classical Buddhist dogmas of reincarnation and the causal chain starting in the ignorance that brought it about were also maintained.

By the middle of the first millennium AD the Mahayanic conceptions outlined above were established alongside the older Hinayana. The religion

44

had also spread beyond the subcontinent into Central Asia along the trade-routes connected with the Silk Road linking China across Xinjiang with the western world. Forms of Buddhism reached China, Japan, Korea by that route and, by others, Sri Lanka, Burma, Thailand, Vietnam and Indonesia. In India, however, Hinduism reasserted itself and was to continue doing so until the disappearance of Buddhism, a consequence only partly due to the Muslim invasions at the turn of the twelfth and thirteenth centuries, for the religions had begun to converge not only in philosophical directions but also in the religious needs of the population. The strongholds of Buddhism from AD 700 became increasingly confined to certain parts of Bihar and Bengal, where the religion began, and to the north-west, particular the Swat Valley and Kashmir. In eastern India there were great monastic complexes often enjoying royal patronage which served as universities and intellectual centres and it is from them that the philosophical and spiritual basis of Tibetan Buddhism was largely and often directly derived.

In the second half of the first millennium the number of images worshipped by Buddhists greatly increased. Ritual became more varied, particularly in the mystical cults whose practices were often a shared if specialised expression of Indian religion. These can be generally described as 'yogic' from a word meaning 'union' (*yoga*) which refers to meditations and practices intended to bring the worshipper into contact with a deity or transcendental principle. The underlying intention, exceedingly old in India, was to annihilate contradictions between god and man; but these practices were now combined with somewhat different methods. On the level of magic yogic practitioners employed spells (*mantras*) for success (*siddhi*) in life as well as for mystical spiritual ends. Specific forms of *yoga* that became common at this period and were adopted by numbers of Buddhists, though by no means all, are described in supposedly secret texts called Tantras and the word Tantrism is therefore used to designate this stage of Buddhism and Hinduism. The word itself can mean 'thread' or 'cord' and may refer to the uninterrupted succession of teachers or initiators who held the key to the often arduous training required of the serious practitioner. Before admission to these cults the postulant received from his teacher an appropriate consecration by which he became qualified to perform certain acts, utter particular spells and place himself in communion with a deity or groups of deities. An early and fundamental example of such groups is the disposition of the five different Buddha forms that appear in Indian sculpture from about the eighth century and earlier in texts. Each of these Buddha images has a different gesture of the hands, is given a special name and associated with a point of the compass, a colour, a virtue as well as a vice and a component of personality according to the Buddhist psychological analysis. In combination these five Buddha figures thus represent the relationship of

18 *Mandala* of Vasudhara, seated in the middle of her emanations, which are concentrically
disposed on lotus petals and contained in a walled square with four gates inside a circle. Outside this
sacred area are gods, holy men and Buddhist symbols. 38½ × 32½ in. 15th–16th century AD.

the idealised universe with the individual. They are emanations or forms of the Absolute as Supreme Buddhahood which, by combining attributes of the universe (macrocosm) with attributes of the individual (microcosm), signify the essential oneness of both. A distribution of deities according to a fixed hierarchic pattern in two or three dimensions to express such relationships was called a *mandala* and as Tantric texts multiplied so did the prescribed combinations for a *mandala*, differing in respect of ritual intention, sectarian affiliation and the visionary experience of the practitioner. The role of the *mandala* in ritual as well as propaganda in the form of sacred pieces of ground made of coloured powders and wall- and cloth-paintings was greatly expanded in Tibet (18). In these *mandalas* we find goddesses or female attendants in the company of major deities and in the sculptural remains and written instructions for Tantric ritual goddesses occur in great number. Their presence may be generally explained by the importance of the female element in the Indian religious world-view. In Buddhism this development created goddesses such as Wisdom personified as Prajnaparamita, or the Perfection of Wisdom, and the saviour goddess Tara, who became especially associated with the compassionate Avalokitesvara (17, 19). In the more specific Tantric context the female principle, identified with transcendental wisdom, or the knowledge of the Absolute as the essential voidness of everything whatsoever, takes on a new role. Unlike the Hindu female principle, she becomes the passive element in conjunction with the ultimate virtue of the Mahayana, compassion, which is the means or method for attaining salvation. The career of the bodhisattva represents it in the classical Mahayana. In Tantric Buddhism the attainment of liberation is conceived of as male compassion acting on, or in conjunction with, female knowledge. These coefficients or elements acting together could be expressed symbolically by sexual union. Representations of deities so joined are found in late Indian Buddhist sculpture which served as models for similar representations in subsequent Tibetan art.

Indian, and after them, Tibetan Tantric texts describe many rites for a variety of spiritual and magical purposes. Their specifically Buddhist application was linked to the quest for illumination and salvation by the rapid path as distinct from that of the earlier Mahayana, which offered the slow path of the bodhisattva with the ripening of the necessary perfections over numerous lives. The rituals of certain classes of Tantra offered the rapid union of the individual with the Absolute by the supernatural power of sound, or mystic formulas and syllables, meditations and sexual acts, symbolic of the unification aimed at. Now Indian religion had come to use rituals in which suitably prepared persons of both sexes performed secret and conventionally immoral acts in token that they were not bound by ordinary spiritual processes and the false restraints of morality. The senses

19 Copper figure of White Tara with a lotus, her left hand in the gesture of giving; she has seven eyes (three on the face and one on each of the palms and soles), a billowing scarf and is seated on the usual lotus-petalled base. Height 11¼ in. 18th century AD.

and not asceticism were exploited for liberation. Such groups – for this was no mass movement – practised consecrations, using *mandalas* for initiations and ritualised sex to express or attain the union or elimination of opposites. This development in Indian religion may have had an orgiastic aspect but it is important to emphasise that the sexual expression of unity could be thought of and performed in wholly symbolic ways. A form of meditation, which was inherited by Tibetan Tantrism, sought the same unity confining it entirely within the body of the meditator. Accordingly two physically fictitious arteries in the body, one on the left, another on the right, represented the polarities or opposites Tantrism was concerned to amalgamate and transcend. By a process of breath control the contents of these arteries, which met at the base of the body, joined a third, central and equally fictitious, artery. There the desire for illumination, symbolised by semen, began its progress up the body until it reached the top of the head and

48

20 (right) *Vajra* or thunderbolt symbol, used ritually with the bell to represent compassion as the means to liberation. Brass, fire gilt. Length 7 in. 19th century AD (?).

21 (far right) Bell (*ghanta*), surmounted by a pronged and gilt brass handle with a crowned head and ornamented with *vajras* and lotus petals containing mystic symbols. Used ritually with the *vajra* to represent supreme knowledge. Height 9 in. 19th century AD (?).

resulted in the Great Bliss of Liberation elsewhere described as attainable by ritual sex. Despite the literalness of Tantric texts and the explicitness of paintings and sculpture their symbolic interpretation prevailed in Tibet and it would be a serious misunderstanding to suppose otherwise.

In this context the use in ritual of the *vajra* or symbol of the thunderbolt or diamond, the emblem of the ancient storm-god Indra and of his Buddhist counterpart Vajrapani, played an important part. A kind of wand, terminating at both ends in converging prongs, it represented the indestructible diamond, the Absolute, voidness and the other terms for the essence Buddhahood. At the same time, in the rituals, it served as the male symbol for the active aspect of compassion as the means to liberation and was held in one hand while in the other was held the symbol of the female pole represented by the bell (20, 21). The word *vajra* came to designate the new Buddhism which was called Vajrayana or the Way of the *Vajra* as the

49

successor of the Mahayana. The two phases or aspects of Buddhism remained, however, closely connected and in Tibet they co-existed, the Mahayana providing the basis of orthodox doctrine, particularly of the Yellow Church, while the Vajrayana was the more specialised doctrine of the rapid path, the practice of which was not always confined to the monasteries. The term Mantrayana, the vehicle or way of the *mantra* ('spell'), or sacred syllable, with its magical power of evoking and compelling divinities, is also used to describe this form of Buddhism.

The development of the Mahayana, the spread of image worship and the elaboration of its philosophical positions occupied roughly the first half of the first millennium AD; the growth of the Vajrayana, or the development of Tantrism, cannot be securely dated for its doctrines were held secret and the names of Tantric authors though known cannot be placed in a dependable chronology. Archaeological remains in what were known to be Tantric centres in northern India before their submergence tend to provide evidence for orthodox practices for the most part but enough survives to link the Tantrism of Tibet firmly with Indian antecedents as literary evidence would require us to believe. Tantric ideas were increasingly characteristic of the second half of the first millennium. The introduction of Buddhism into Tibet was soon affected by them and there is reason to think that foreign influences, Tibetan included, affected Indian Tantrism. The beginnings of Tibetan Buddhism, a long evangelisation from India, are divided into a 'First Diffusion' (between AD 627–842), followed by a period of obscurity, and a 'Second Diffusion' (from about 978) which so securely established Buddhism that when its Indian source all but disappeared after 1200 Tibetan Buddhism was able to maintain itself without dependence on renewal from any outside source.

The Tibetan histories attribute the beginnings of First Diffusion to the great king Srong-brtsan-sgam-po (*c*. AD 627–650) under whom several temples were founded, including the Jo-khang or cathedral of Lhasa, which still stands today, though much added to. The introduction did not penetrate at all deeply into Tibetan life; patronage may have been confined to the court under the influence of the king's Buddhist wives, one Nepalese, the other Chinese. His successors were not notably fervent for the faith until the reign of Khri-srong-lde-brtsan (755–797) when Buddhism became a far stronger force. In certain respects the dynasty remained faithful to ancient native religious practices but as rulers of a newly unified state, fighting China for paramountcy in Central Asia, they may have tried to use the foreign religion as a unifying political and civilising instrument. Under Khri-srong-lde-brtsan two notable Indian evangelists worked in Tibet, one, Santarakshita, representing the orthodox monastic tradition, the other, Padmasambhava, a mystic and magician, who brought the traditions and

50

22 Gilt figure of Padmasambhava, an 8th-century Tantric evangelist, who is said to have tamed demons, obliging them to become protector gods. He is seated and holds the vase of life in a skull cup in one hand and a *vajra* in the other. Height 15 in. 18th century AD.

practices of Tantrism from Uddiyana, which is perhaps to be identified with the Swat Valley in modern Pakistan (22). To Santarakshita is attributed the foundation of the first monastery (temples only had existed until then) at bSam-yas (10) in about AD 779, which is said to have been built in imitation of a famous Indian foundation, Uddandapura, whose site cannot now be identified. Padmasambhava, on the other hand, is credited with the subjugation of demons and hostile spirits whom he converted into protectors of the faith thus beginning a process which gave a place in the Tibetan Buddhist pantheon for many of the fierce and grotesque local deities who form such a striking feature of it. According to rNying-ma-pa tradition, Padmasambhava hid numerous texts which were rediscovered when that sect, which claims spiritual descent from him, took shape. During the same reign a controversy developed between Chinese Buddhist adherents of the rapid path of Buddhahood and Indian defenders of the classical Mahayana or bodhisattva progression by stages. A public debate took place and the Mahayanists were declared the winners. Under king Ral-pa-can (815–838) Buddhism was still more favoured and important progress was made in translating Buddhist books into an acceptable Tibetan idiom. The king's devotion to Buddhism and his economic favour to the monasteries exacerbated the conflict between the royal family and the nobility who continued to support the native religion. He was soon murdered and his brother Glang-dar-ma (838–842) led a reaction against Buddhism which, despite his assassination at the hand of a Buddhist monk, effectively reduced the religion to an insignificant position in the years of political turmoil that followed. It does not appear, however, that between 842 and its revival in the late tenth century all trace of the religion vanished and it is likely that popular cults, and more specifically the Bon-po, exercised considerable influence while Buddhism was deprived of royal patronage, supervision from monastic intellectual centres and the authority of Indian teachers. Tantric ritual in its more explicitly sexual forms is said to have found adherents at this time. Influences in the opposite direction, which began to make the old Bon something much closer to Buddhism were probably also active during this period.

Buddhist monasticism appears to have survived in eastern Tibet and was revived in Lhasa by monks from that region in about 978. It was not long before patronage by aristocratic and feudal lords led to the establishment of new monasteries which remained linked to the founding family by economic and dynastic ties. This was a vital feature in the expansion of Tibetan monasticism, which in this way became an element of government in the country, culminating in the rule of the Dalai Lamas. Another powerful source for the renewal of Buddhism was the active patronage of the western Tibetan kings, who were descendants of the old central monarchs and retained the tradition of favouring Buddhism. One of them, Ye-shes-'od, became a monk himself. It was during his lifetime that Rin-chen bzang-po (958–1055), who visited India several times and is credited with religious foundations in the western Tibetan kingdom of Gu-ge as well as many translations of Buddhist texts, did much to revive Buddhism. Under the impact of his activity Buddhism was strengthened in central Tibet also and both regions were visited by the Indian scholar Atisa between 1042–54; he died and is buried at sNye-thang. The work of Atisa is marked by a great strengthening of the monastic tradition and its disciplines, but in common with all the teachers, both Indian and Tibetan, over the next two centuries he accepted, though in their symbolic and esoteric forms, the Indian Tantric teachings, practices and meditations that the Tibetans found particularly to their taste. Through his pupil 'Brom-ston (1004–64), who founded the monastery of Reting (Rva-sgreng), Atisa counts as the source of one of the many traditions or sects, which with the exception of the rNying-ma-pa, or followers of Padmasambhava, owe their beginnings to the different Indian and Tibetan personalities active during the Second Diffusion and the monasteries where the special emphases of their teachings were institutionalised. The tradition deriving from Atisa, the bKa'-gdams-pa, was noted for its moral strictness which, with other conservative features, formed the basis for the reforms of Tsong-kha-pa (1357–1419) who founded the tradition of the Yellow Hats. It was this sect which came to dominate Tibetan Buddhism and provided its apparatus of government under the Dalai Lamas.

It is, however, necessary to emphasise that even when they ruled Tibet, the Yellow Hats had not suppressed the other traditions of Tibetan Buddhism and some of them, already mentioned in a political context, may again be briefly referred to here. During the Second Diffusion many Tibetans travelled to India to study at the great monastic universities, destroyed around AD 1200, and to be initiated into various Tantric traditions and Indians, in much smaller numbers, came to teach in Tibet. The result was a variety of method due to the competing authority of the different Indian masters from whom the sectarian traditions stemmed. This variety led to a great richness, for these traditions did not flow in isolated channels but constantly influenced each other. (One may mention as transcending sect the *bar-do* beliefs and the principles of Naropa, one of the best-known sectarian masters.) It was by no means uncommon for members of different sects to live in the same monastery. Preference might be given to one tutelary deity over another and different combinations of deities with their attendant rituals might be resorted to, but so long as the disciplinary differences were not too great such a co-existence was not unlike what was reported of Indian monastic life many centuries earlier.

Even the rNying-ma-pa, mentioned above as antedating the Second Diffusion, followers of the older Tantras and venerating Padmasambhava as a second Buddha eclipsing the historical Buddha, cannot be regarded as preserving an uncontaminated tradition from the earlier diffusion. The 'rediscovery' during the Second Diffusion and later of scriptures (*gter-ma*), said to have been concealed by Padmasambhava, points rather to a reconstitution of the older tradition that had nevertheless been clearly affected, no doubt particularly between the First and Second Diffusions, by elements from the aboriginal religions. For their adherence to these apocryphal texts as well as for their veneration of Padmasambhava, the rNying-ma-pa are reproached by other sects. The rNying-ma-pa follow Tantric texts of a magical character traditionally revealed by goddesses called *dakinis*; there are numerous exorcists amongst them and they are said not to abstain from animal sacrifices. The number of aboriginal deities accepted by them is much greater than with other schools and like the Bon-po they divide their scriptures into a nine-fold grouping and give the same name to their Supreme Buddha as the Bon-po to their high god of White Light. Monasteries of this sect still exist outside political Tibet.

A very productive tradition is that of the bKa'-rgyud-pa which has split into a number of sub-sects, one of which, the 'Brug-pa, are the dominant sect in Bhutan today. Their teachings derive from the *siddhas* (pl. 12), individualistic Indian Tantrists who were themselves not always in the monastic tradition. They emphasise certain forms of *yoga,* breathing exercises, the use of *mantras* and the generation of bodily heat by the concentration of the thought of enlightenment into the imagined central artery of the meditator's body and its progress to the top of the head. This is one of Naropa's principles, mentioned above as having become part of the general practice of Tibetan Buddhist *yoga.* Its efficacy is reflected in the life of Mi-la ras-pa (1040–1123), a well-known ascetic and poet, whose verses have survived as part of the general Tibetan heritage and are widely quoted. Warmed by the inner fire of this ascetic practice, he wore no more than a light cotton garment even in the depth of the Tibetan winter. Another of the principles of Naropa, an Indian *siddha* from whom the bKa'-rgyud-pa are spiritually descended, is the *bar-do* or the intermediate state between physical death and the next birth or liberation. The practices of preparing oneself for its visions and being instructed during it by readings from the 'Book of the Dead' have spread beyond the sectarian limits of the bKa'-rgyud-pa. Politically the sub-sect of the 'Bri-gung was important as opponents of the Sa-skya-pa and another, the Phag-mo-gru, replaced the Sa-skya hegemony.

The most prominent predecessors of the dGe-lugs-pa as rulers of Tibet were the Sa-skya-pa sect, whose first monastery was founded in AD 1073. Their doctrines concerned the relationship of thought or mind, which had a luminous nature, with the void or Absolute, which was the essence of thought. This doctrine was a development of the Yogacara philosophy of the Indian Mahayana. The Sa-skya-pa continued to exist after their brief political dominance during the Yuan Mongol period (1260–1368). Their tutelary deity was Hevajra and it was by the Tantric ritual of this deity that Kublai Khan was initiated. An unusual feature of the Sa-skya-pa tradition is that its abbots were permitted to marry.

An important doctrinal text, the *Kalacakra*, achieved considerable status in Tibet where it was introduced about 1026. Apart from its great interest for chronology and astrology, for the Tibetan calendar was based on it, the *Kalacakra* system stressed the concept of the Adi Buddha, or Primordial Buddha (23). Several sects adopted this embodied version of the *Dharmakaya*, or Body of the Doctrine, which had been thought of as the Absolute beyond all form and rational apprehension. The Adi Buddha of the Yellow Hats and of the bKa'-rgyud-pa was called Vajradhara or Vajrasattva, that of the rNying-ma-pa was Samantabhadra.

23 Vajradhara, the Primordial Buddha, with wrists crossed, holding the *vajra* and bell; he has silver inlaid eyes and ornaments, with copper inlay and incised decoration on the garments. Brass. Height 9½ in. 15th–16th century AD.

GODS OF TIBETAN BUDDHISM

With its inheritance of Indian deities and those added in the centuries of development in Tibet, the pantheon of Lamaism is so large that existing accounts fall far short of being exhaustive. The literary sources have still to be fully explored and our knowledge of the images and paintings is still incomplete. It must be borne in mind that in using the word pantheon we refer not to a single orthodox grouping valid for the whole of Tibetan Buddhism in its widest sense. The forms of deities differed between schools or sects and on a popular level large numbers of local gods and demons had been absorbed into a more or less Buddhist context. Tantric ritual in India resulted in a great specialisation of iconographic forms over a long period. In the end the Tantric practices and deities may have been understood as symbols, with visionary meditation contributing new entities or variants, but at the time of their compositon the Tantras were absorbing Hindu gods and popular deities as well as practices from esoteric or mystery cults. It is rather the formation of many pantheons, though with shared elements, that characterised the growth of Tantrism.

The Tibetan deities and figures worshipped were drawn from Buddhas, bodhisattvas, goddesses, the special tutelary gods presiding over sects, monasteries and individuals, defenders of the faith who included great, fierce and terrible gods as well as more modest local spirits, gods of the cardinal points, saints from early Buddhist tradition, later philosophers, teachers, kings and wonder-workers. The thirteenth Dalai Lama, who died in 1933, and was an incarnation of Avalokitesvara, was commemorated in effigy, to which offerings were made.

Iconography, the study of the features that distinguish the form of one deity from another, is thus a particularly necessary part of the study of Tibetan sculpture and painting. Fortunately, Indian and Tibetan tradition have preserved many texts which describe and name gods either singly or disposed in groups according to a specific order for various ritual purposes. These texts not only give us meditation processes by which gods were summoned out of their mystic syllables but minutely detail their postures, colours, clothing, ornaments and the objects they held in their hands. These attributes are very numerous and, since Indian tradition had already established that the power of gods was expressed by a multiplicity of arms and heads, the permutations available to its Tibetan successor were so great that the Lamaist pantheon achieved a complexity unrivalled in any other religion (24). It can be hard to identify a deity correctly yet it must be remembered that the form in question was fixed according to rules that might not be disregarded. To the newcomer such figures may sometimes seem alien to the point of repulsion, and bewilderment is not diminished by

24 (left) Guhyasamaja, a tutelary deity seated in embrace with his female partner. Each has three heads and six arms. The figures are of silver, the ornaments and attributes, the latter separately cast, are gilt. Height 6 in. 18th century AD.

25 (right) Simhavaktra, the lion-headed *dakini* with chopper and blood-filled skull cap, and garlanded with snakes and freshly severed human heads. Brass. Height 5in. 18th century AD.

the convention of showing many gods in close sexual embrace with female partners and adopting fierce and terrible forms, part human, part animal (25). From the Buddhist point of view, these representations are symbols of the highest importance. In the sexual form they stand for the components of liberation: knowledge and compassion joined to achieve the elimination of all opposites. The fierce and wrathful aspects are symbols of the power that brings the aspirant to liberation and protects him against the dangers on that path. Meditation on such deities and their entourage is an intense and

26 *Karttrika* or chopper carried by many fierce deities and said to cut the life-roots of enemies and demons. Brass, fire gilt. Height 7 in. 19th century AD.

arduous progression by which one may become identified with the Absolute. In this function the fierce deities are manifestations of that Absolute in one of its emanatory forms. But they do not always serve the same exalted end. Some classes of ritual use them on a magical level not as guides on the way to salvation but as powers to gain other ends: subduing, exorcising, making rain, slaying, propitiating, winning a woman, finding something that was lost and so on. Another source of disquiet may be found in the attributes of these fierce gods, for many of them also express aggression and death. Common attributes are knives, daggers, skull cups and drums, bone trumpets, garlands and wands with skulls or severed heads and flayed human and animal skins. They can now all be referred to a consistent symbolism, as we shall see, but in origin they must at least in part go back to cults involving cemetery rituals, for in India a cemetery or burning ground was thought a particularly suitable place for the ascetic to overcome natural human instincts connected with the illusory concepts of pleasure, pain and the vanities of life. The Buddha himself is said to have meditated in cemeteries to achieve this kind of indifference on his way to Enlightenment. To eat and drink from a skull, to live amongst corpses and to brave the physical and emotional dangers of the charnel house were a recognised technique of asceticism. That gods should carry emblems symbolising the conquest of such fears was thus wholly compatible with spiritual endeavour. These gods, like all phenomena, were in the final instance illusory and valueless except as transmuted into symbols by which fears, evil, hatred and cruelty were accorded their place in a world characterised by suffering and put into the service of the quest for liberation.

In the following account the peaceful and fierce deities will to some extent

58

be treated separately, an approach with a certain historical justification, but it should not be allowed to obscure the Tibetan view that emanation from the Absolute underlies all phenomena and that fierce deities are often a specific manifestation for which a peaceful equivalent is also recognised.

The classical early *mandala* carried over from India into Tibet was based on the emanative character of buddhahood which provided a group of transcendent Buddhas between the phenomenal world and the principle of buddhahood as the Absolute, which was equated either with the principle of voidness or of universal consciousness. This group, originally five, consisted of Buddhas of the centre and the four cardinal points, each distinguishable by a gesture and possessing a separate name. They were the heads of families with many members, an important iconographic consideration, for these families had emblems and a distinguishing colour whose use in a given context had to be invariable. These five Buddhas are often called Dhyani Buddhas or Buddhas of Meditation (27). This expression has no known textual justification and is due to Brian Hodgson, British resident in Kathmandu in the early nineteenth century who may nevertheless have

27 Ratnasambhava, one of the five Dhyani Buddhas, crowned and ornamented and with his right hand in the gesture of giving. Stalks on both sides join ribbons projecting from the crown. Brass. Height 9 in. 16th century AD.

heard or read it. The expression is still widely used and is therefore convenient but the texts refer to Jinas and Tathagatas. From the concept of a central Tathagata in the *mandalas* as well as the notion of a Supreme Buddha principle beyond the five manifestations, an Adi Buddha or Primordial Buddha was evolved, usually called Vajradhara or Vajrasattva but Samantabhadra among the rNying-ma-pa. Vajradhara and Vajrasattva are also equated with the zenith and nadir respectively.

These Adi and Dhyani Buddhas can appear with consorts as well as alone; the Adi Buddhas always wear crowns and ornaments while the Tathagatas vary in this respect; they do so when joined with their partners in sexual embrace, but singly can still have the classical monastic appearance of the historical Buddha with plain robe and no ornaments. The transition from the early iconography of the monastic Buddha to an ornamented and crowned figure is probably to be connected with the evolution of the doctrine of the Three Bodies which distinguished from the so-called historical Buddha the Buddhas of Meditation who in turn were manifestations of Buddhahood in its absolute form.

Some of the most important deities were those that acted as tutelaries or guarantors (*yi-dam*) through whom the Tantric practitioner attained spiritual powers and identification with Buddhahood. The *yi-dam* was thus an individual's particular deity and usually chosen for him by his teacher or lama. The choice might be governed by the spiritual needs of the individual or dictated by the affiliation of the monastery or sect to which one or other belonged. Sometimes a *yi-dam* was chosen by throwing a flower on to a *mandala* laid out on the floor of the temple and the deity on whom it fell became the *yi-dam*. Selection by the lama involved a judgement of personality, for the Tathagatas and their familes represented or presided over vices and it was through the transformation of those into the appropriate Tathagata's wisdom or quality that the mystic progressed towards ultimate identification with the Absolute. This selection was also made in dreams or by some other mystic sign.

The process by which the meditator invoked a special deity to achieve power or spiritual advance fell into two parts. The first began with rites justifying the purpose of the meditation and a purification of the practitioner. Then followed an act of mental creation. Conscious of the void nature of reality, the meditator drew out from the deity's mystic syllable the physical presence of the deity, its attributes and, where appropriate, its attendants, mentally piecing the whole together with the utmost precision. The deity became simultaneously present in the meditator's vision as something separate from himself and identical with him. As something separate it received worship, acted for the salvation of others or exercised its powers on the meditator's behalf for more mundane ends. The second part

60

28 Vajrabhairava, a form of Yamantaka and tutelary of the Yellow Church, with nine heads, thirty-four arms and sixteen legs, embracing his partner and standing on gods and animals. Hammered brass, fire gilt. Height 19 in. From a temple in Peking and dated to AD 1811.

of the meditation involved an opposite process; the deity and its entourage, the apparently objective creation, were dissassembled or dismissed and the physical evocation, which could have the full complexity of a *mandala* or paradise painting, returned into its void nature. This process of creation and reabsorption would enable the practitioner, if this was his purpose, to experience the illusion of phenomenal reality, detach himself from it and attain union with the Absolute.

To gauge something of the difficulty of this process as well as understand the symbolic function of a god's attributes we may refer to a meditational description of the tutelary god Vajrabhairava. It begins with a physical enumeration of his colour, nine faces, thirty-four arms and sixteen feet. He is credited with the power of swallowing the three worlds, frightening even the most terrifying gods, eating flesh, human fat and drinking blood. The flames issuing from his face and body are compared with those of the universal conflagration when the cosmos undergoes one of its traditional periodic dissolutions. Then his attributes are described in terms of their efficacy against illusion. Some have a more or less obvious symbolism: the knife destroys ignorance, the razor sin, the axe mental error, the spear mistaken views and the club the ignorance induced by the effect of past actions. His threatening hand frightens demons, his noose binds together Supreme Knowledge and his trident indicates that the planes of the spirit, the word and the body are not essentially different. Other attributes have a far less obvious relationship with what they stand for. The magic wand expresses the identity of the god's nature with the Thought of Enlightenment; the drum, as equivalent of Supreme Bliss, unifies the five Buddhas of Meditation; the blood-filled skull cup stimulates fidelity to the vow; the severed head of a Hindu god signifies the pity that impels Vajrabhairava to concern himself with the welfare of all living things; another freshly severed head shows that he possesses the compassionate food of immortality; the foot signifies that the meditator has equal rank with the Buddhas; the impaled body means that he understands that nothing has any independent nature; a piece of cloth shows that all is illusion and the beings that he treads upon symbolise his mystic powers.

Most of the deities already described can be used as *yi-dam*, though they are considered at their most effective when paired with their female partners as a *yab-yum* couple. Thus *yi-dam* may be peaceful Tathagatas, bodhisattvas and goddesses as well as fierce and special manifestations like the one just described.

A particularly rich and productive category of deities in Tibet is that of the dharmapalas, or guardians of the faith, who are nearly all fierce for their function is to protect the Buddhist doctrine and its practice. Legend claims that dharmapalas were originally hostile local demons of Tibet who were

62

tamed by Padmasambhava, the Tantric master and early evangelist of the eighth century, and compelled to watch over the Buddhist religion. There is also a group of eight mainly Indian 'Terrible Ones', some having numerous forms; but many other deities have guardian status and as Padmasambhava tamed hostile forces in his own time, so later teachers are said to have continued to bring local gods and spirits into the Lamaist fold by taming them and binding them by oath to undertake the protection of the religion and of specific monasteries. They and their attendants became especially numerous and were worshipped in a separate shrine in the monasteries.

The outline given above has attempted to fit the chief gods of Lamaism into the structure of the doctrine of emanations, the Tantric systems with their organisation by *mandalas* and the functional distribution into tutelaries and protectors. Works on Tibetan iconography commonly distribute deities under a greater number of headings without necessarily specifying affiliations and some of these gods may be briefly summarised here.

In addition to the tranquil Buddhas already mentioned there are Buddhas of Medicine whose function speaks for itself; with the historical Buddha they form a group of eight. Another group consists of thirty-five Buddhas of Confession while a group of six presides over each of the six states of existence into which a living being can be reborn. The bodhisattvas, like the Buddhas, are originally peaceful but their numbers and forms have grown; they are divided among different Buddha families and they too have fierce aspects. Among goddesses are independent deities with the rank of bodhisattva, such as Tara; a group of five protective goddesses inherited from India and personifying spells; the *dakinis* who are both consorts of *yi-dams* and initiation goddesses, granting superhuman powers (29); the goddesses of the seasons; the Five Sisters of Long Life and eight personified goddesses of the ritual offerings. Lamaism also absorbed many Hindu gods, often shown underneath the Buddhist deities, serpent spirits from Indian and Tibetan tradition, as well as gods of wealth and the guardians of the cardinal points (30). The country gods are a variety of popular spirits, belonging to the folk tradition accepted by Buddhism and clearly local in origin. They are mountain, earth and house gods. The deities of the *bar-do*, seen during the intermediate period following death, include, as well as more familiar Buddhist gods, groups of indigenous origin.

Deified legendary and historical figures range from supposed disciples of the Buddha (the group of sixteen *arhats* often shown with their two companions), philosophers who codified the doctrines of developed Buddhism, Indian *siddhas* and their Tibetan successors, Buddhist evangelists in Tibet, Tibetan abbots, founders of sectarian traditions and Dalai Lamas.

29 (left) *Dakini* in dancing posture with chopper and skull cup; a *khatvanga* wand may have rested on her left shoulder. Her parent Buddha, Akshobhya, appears on the head-dress. Copper figure with silver inlay on brass base. Height 6½ in. 17th century AD.

30 (right) Gilt copper figure of Dhritarashtra, one of the four guardians of the points of the compass, who watches over the eastern entrance of Amitabha's paradise; he holds a stringed instrument. His helmet is plumed and his armour partly made of small plaques sewn together. Height 8 in. 18th century AD.

INCARNATIONS

A striking feature of Lamaism, especially in its later period, when a celibate monkhood became an instrument of government, was the use of the principle of reincarnation as a form of spiritual and political succession. Heads of monasteries were appointed by virtue of their being recognised as incarnations of their predecessors, a system that goes back to Dus-gsum-mkhyen-pa (1110–93), first head of the Karma-pa branch of the bKa'-rgyud-pa sect, who prophesied his reincarnation as his own successor. Such prophecies were to be an important means of identifying reincarnations who, as infants, were expected to show certain qualifying signs. Monasteries of many sects adopted the system of regularly reincarnating lamas to secure the succession of their abbots. The best-known example is of course its application to the government of Tibet between the seventeenth century and our own day, when the Dalai Lamas, originally abbots and sectarian heads, were the rulers of Tibet.

An earlier conception of occasional reincarnation may be seen in the rNying-ma-pa tradition where its founder, Padmasambhava, or his disciples

31 Summer hat of laquered papier-mâché worn by incarnates out of doors. Decorated with flower and leaf patterns, Buddhist symbols and dragons. Height 8 in.; diameter 16 in. 19th century AD.

were considered to take on human form only when it was necessary to find hidden writings and give correct interpretations of corrupted teachings.

By far the largest number of regular reincarnations were explained as those of specific individuals whose spiritual ascent had brought them to the threshold of buddhahood, i.e., as bodhisattvas who, faithful to Mahayanist ethic, then chose to return to this world to exercise a saviour's function until all beings had been brought to Enlightenment. A distinction between incarnations of Indian and Tibetan saints or teachers gave the higher rank to the former. But it was the successors of the Tibetans who provided the hundreds of incarnations who held the dignity of abbot, being recognised in childhood as the immediate reincarnations of their predecessors and brought up from an early age in the monasteries, though often with little or no administrative responsibility. A monastery might indeed contain more than one incarnate but an incarnate did not necessarily have to be a monk or an abbot or even celibate.

Some incarnations were believed to be of special deities of the Buddhist pantheon. The great Bodhisattva of Wisdom, Manjusri (32), is said to have incarnated himself seven times in the founding family of the first Sa-skya monastery (AD 1073) and Tsong-kha-pa (1357–1419), the spiritual founder of the Yellow Hat sect, was also regarded as an incarnation of Manjusri. The abbess of bSam-lding monastery and convent was claimed regularly to incarnate the goddess Vajravarahi and the Panchen Lama of Tashilhunpo was the Tathagata or Dhyani Buddha Amitabha.

The most important reincarnation was of course the Dalai Lama. In 1578 the Mongol ruler Altan Khan conferred the title of Dalai Lama on bSod-nams rGya-mtsho (1543–88), third in a dGe-lugs-pa incarnation series starting with dGe-'dun-grub (1391–1475), who had been one of Tsong-kha-pa's disciples. The title was retrospectively given to the two earlier abbots. All three, with the Dalai Lamas, their successors, were subsequently held to incarnate the compassionate saviour god and Bodhisattva Avalokitesvara, who was also the traditional patron deity of Tibet. Avalokitesvara's supposed incarnations indeed went back to the mythical monkey ancestor of the Tibetan people and continued into historical times with such figures as kings of unified Tibet in the seventh and eighth centuries and religious leaders before the dGe-lugs-pa reforms. Avalokitesvara was not himself directly incarnated afresh with each birth: every successive individual was the rebirth of his predecessor and Avalokitesvara himself appears only at the start of this lineage. At the same time he was supposed to be present in an appropriate Buddhist heaven. A similar principle held with the other incarnations of Buddhist deities such as the second most important abbot of Tibet, the Panchen Lama: each successive hierarch was the rebirth of his predecessor; historically the first of the Panchen series was the fifth Dalai

Lama's teacher, Blo-bzang Chos-kyi rGyal-mtshan (1569–1662), whom the Dalai Lama installed as abbot of the dGe-lugs-pa stronghold of Tashilhunpo proclaiming him an incarnation of Amitabha. But his succession was also extended backwards into a mythical series.

The recognition of a Dalai Lama was in principle determined by the same method as the discovery of any other incarnation. But the political and material implications connected with such a powerful position led to greater efforts to ensure the discovery of the right child and to eliminate corruption. Like other incarnates a Dalai Lama might himself indicate before his death where he would be reborn, giving details to aid the search. Oracles were consulted by abbots of the greater monasteries and enquiries made as to whether exceptional children had been reported. Such children were examined for physical marks to connect them with Avalokitesvara, such as indications of a tiger skin on the legs, hints near the shoulder-blades of a second pair of arms, imprints suggesting a conch shell on the palms, long ears and long and upward-curving eyes and eyebrows. Another test was to show the candidates ritual implements that had belonged to the previous Dalai Lama along with others indistingishable from them and see which was picked. Accounts have been published of the discovery of the thirteenth Dalai Lama (1876–1933) by his friend, Sir Charles Bell, and of the present incumbent (1935–   ) by his elder brother, Thubten Jigme Norbu, who also

32 Manjusri, the Bodhisattva of Wisdom, with the sword that destroys ignorance on the lotus at his right shoulder and the book of wisdom in the form of a palm-leaf volume at his left. Copper figure with gold inlay. Height 5½ in. 14th century AD.

67

tells of his own recognition as an incarnate and his appointment to a wealthy monastery in his native Amdo. In the case of the present Dalai Lama the choice was apparently aided by his otherwise inexplicable command over official court language.

In order to keep some control over the appointment of a Dalai Lama the Chinese in 1793 prescribed selection by lottery, using a golden urn to pick out a name with a pair of chopsticks in the presence of the Chinese Resident. It is said that whenever the urn was used, the name withdrawn was that already favoured by the oracles. The urn was not used in the discovery of the thirteenth Dalai Lama though a lottery was resorted to in the last selection. The temptation for Tibetans to falsify incarnations could be great for some 'livings' were very rich and a Dalai Lama's family was ennobled and given estates. For the Chinese it was expedient to have control over the Tibetan ruler not least because of his great religious authority over their turbulent Mongol neighbours.

MONASTERIES

Although the introduction of Buddhism into Tibet is put between *c.* AD 627 and 650 under Srong-brtsan-sgam-po, the first great king of the centralised monarchy, it appears that only temples were erected between that time and the reign of Khri-srong-lde-brtsan (*c.* AD 755–797).

The organised monastic settlements, which must have played a large part in the successful spread of the religion in and beyond India by the time of the First Diffusion, existed in large numbers in India and Central Asia as literature and archaeology prove. Their absence in Tibet may reinforce doubts about the strength of Buddhist penetration at this very early period. After the foundation of the temple-monastery of bSam-yas (*c.* 779) under royal patronage, however, monasteries rapidly became economically very powerful and challenged the feudal nobility, thus no doubt strengthening its loyalty to the old religion and increasing its hostility to the centralising ambitions of the royal house. Tibetan documents of that period describe the generous endowments to the monasteries and give a foretaste of what, after the eclipse of the religion between 842 and 978, was to become the regular pattern, later endowments being made either by lesser princelings or the nobility who, now Buddhist and formally no doubt acting in accordance with the orthodox motivations of acquiring merit by good works, tried to harness the monastic movement to their own interests.

By the twentieth century monasteries and, to a lesser extent, nunneries were established throughout Tibet; there were probably more than 3,000,

68

33 View along the rooftops of Tashilhunpo monastery, near Shigatse, with the characteristic dark painted twig walling, pitched roofs and banner finials. The high building was used as a storehouse and to display hangings with Buddhas. (Photo H. E. Richardson)

ranging from small establishments with a few buildings, including a temple, an assembly-hall and living quarters for its inmates, to huge cities, with populations of many thousands of monks, which reflected in part the university character of some of the great foundations of India. In them monks worshipped, studied and meditated or managed the often considerable property of the monastery while others may have done very little at all, for recruitment to the order was part of the traditional social pattern, especially in the settled regions and rarely reflected an individual's sense of vocation. The greater monasteries were more or less strictly organised but most of them were run along far looser lines with considerable freedom for the monks to follow individual spiritual inclinations, reading, writing, performing priestly duties in the villages or becoming involved in family affairs, especially if there was a traditional connection between the monastery and their family. In such cases the residential cell or residence was already their property. Monasteries therefore differed in size, educational and political importance and sectarian emphases. The description that follows only attempts to summarise some characteristic features.

Architecturally the monastery was essentially a Tibetan building or complex of these. Built of stones or sun-dried bricks the walls often sloped inwards and the roofs, except those of the assembly-halls, were flat, a feature already reported of Tibetan building in the Chinese annals of the Tang dynasty (AD 618–907). The pitched and tiered roofs seen on the Potala and above the main halls of monastic buildings were ornamental and were due to Chinese influence.

The usually flat roof of wooden beams supported by pillars with characteristic bracket capitals reflected a climate with low rainfall (34). The windows sometimes narrowed towards the top and the roofs had parapets, gold cylinders representing the banner of victory and finials with tridents. Below there was sometimes willow twig walling several feet high and painted a dull red, against which were attached circular gold or gilt emblems.

Simple and early temples were small rectangular buildings with a covered verandah or portico entrance with the image opposite surrounded by a small passage for ritual circumambulation. In the later chapels of the greater monasteries the image was rarely alone and stood against the far wall above the altar. The hall itself was divided into aisles by wooden pillars. The lighting from outside was provided from the portico, through an opening in the ceiling or by a clerestory. Where chapels and assembly-rooms were on an upper foor the lighting was provided by windows. In the porticoes there were paintings or images representing the Kings of the Four Quarters, the Wheel of Life – a painted statement of the Buddhist law of causality – and other paintings as well as large prayer-barrels. Inside the walls were painted with *mandalas*, figures of gods, saints and demons. The wooden pillars were

71

34 View of part of the courtyard of the chapel at Glang-thang, north of Lhasa. (Photo H. E. Richardson)

swathed in cloth, wrapped round with rugs, painted and hung with banners and embroidered pennants.

The rest of the monastery was spread around the central temple and assembly-hall. The basic unit was an open courtyard surrounded by buildings of several storeys fronted with passages or cloisters. These courtyards were separated from other buildings or complexes by streets. The larger teaching monastery contained not only a central temple and assembly-hall but also, with the surrounding residential quarters, colleges with their own chapels, forming a number of separate economic units with considerable autonomy and their own administration. These were almost separate monasteries and sometimes had a regional character: the large monasteries or mother-houses were responsible for the expenses of monks from branch monasteries who could not complete their education for want of facilities at the lesser houses. Such colleges and dormitories received gifts from wealthy patrons, and monks were also supported by scholarships. Much of the space also was given over to store-rooms for the considerable quantities of food, especially the butter, tea and barley, with which the monks had to be continually supplied during ceremonies which could be exceedingly long.

Especially in the larger monasteries there were a number of daily assemblies at which the monks, summoned by bells, large drums and the sounding of conch-shell trumpets, sat in rows at right angles to the altar, facing each other across the central passage. These services, especially in the large Yellow Hat monasteries, were sternly supervised for decorum by specially appointed monks. At these services meditations on the tutelary deities took place, prayers were addressed to the protectors of the Doctrine, and appropriate recitations were accompanied by the use of *vajra* and bell and bell and hand-drum; when a deity was invoked all the instruments, conches, trumpets, shawms, cymbals and drums were sounded. If required, prayers were offered in the course of daily assemblies for the sick or dead, to avert disasters and exorcise demons. There were also general assemblies for specific feast days such as those connected with the New Year, the winter Festival of the Doctrine, events in the Buddha's career and occasions of special meaning to the sect to which the monastery belonged. Thus the rNying-ma-pa celebrated the life of Padmasambhava and the Sa-skya-pa their special tutelary god Hevajra. A particular monastery might also commemorate its previous head-lama. Special rites of exorcism or those for the particular spiritual or material welfare of an individual also brought the monks together. Common to all these assemblies was the provision at frequent intervals of tea and food brought to the assembly-hall by lay servants but distributed within only by novices. A layman might always gain merit by paying for special ceremonies; the merit increased in proportion to

I

2

1 The outer face of a carved, painted and gilt wooden book-cover. In the centre is Manjusri, the Bodhisattva of Wisdom, with the Primordial Buddha Vajrasattva on his right and the saviour goddess Tara on his left. $10\frac{3}{4} \times 29$ in. 17th century AD.

2 The inner painted face of a wooden book-cover. In the central compartment is the goddess of Transcendent Wisdom (Prajnaparamita). The nine compartments at both sides contain deities and monks. $10\frac{5}{8} \times 28\frac{1}{2}$ in. 15th century AD.

3 Monk's jacket of red wool with silk facing round the collar and on the front edges. It is partially decorated with patchwork using different coloured silk brocades with floral patterns. Height 30 in. 19th–20th century AD.

4 Long sleeveless garment for actresses or actors playing female parts in strolling troupes. Strips of plain brown silk alternate with strips of silk brocade with floral patterns in various colours. Height 46 in. 19th–20th century AD.

5 Copper tea-pot on a gilt stand. It is richly decorated with gilding and silverwork. The handle and silver spout are in the form of dragons. Other decorative features include heavenly musicians and Buddhist symbols. Height 13 in. 19th century AD.

6 The bull-headed Yama, the ancient Indian god of death and one of the eight great protectors of Buddhism. Surrounded by flames, he holds a skull-topped wand and a noose. Embroidery. $25\frac{3}{4} \times 18$ in. 18th century AD.

the outlay on the butter and flour for the sacrificial cakes, the feeding of butter lamps and quantities of butter tea, rice, soup and other food provided for the monks.

In their educational functions the monasteries varied according to their sect, for the schools differed in the emphases placed on doctrinal and liturgical practices on the one hand and mystical experience on the other. Even though the latter might be considered the final or most effective way of achieving spiritual liberation the educational requirements still emphasised the value of formal academic attainment in the inherited body of doctrinal and liturgical knowledge. Beyond these lay the complexities of Tantra and the mastery not merely of their texts but also the controlled visionary and psychological practices they inculcated. A period of five years was allotted to the first set of studies; the second might take seven or more in the monasteries where particular importance was attached to them. Such would be establishments of the rNying-ma-pa and bKa'-rgyud-pa; a feature of the dGe-lugs-pa curriculum was the emphasis placed on logic and the art of formal disputation. The sects also differed as to the qualifications to be gained from the courses of study in the monasteries.

The educational grades were not always the same as the stages by which a monk advanced within the order. There were three stages in the ordination and they depended on the number of vows from the ancient disciplinary code that were taken. The first stage, corresponding to that of the lay brother in Indian tradition could be, and often was, entered by a child of about eight or under who put on monastic robes, acquired a new name in religion and began his religious education with the elements of literacy. In this capacity, unless his family were able to support him, he also acted as a servitor to an older monk who became his teacher. After about two years the boy entered the next stage which was that of *dge-tshul* and required the taking of 36 vows. This stage involved further training and education and was properly that of the novice. From about the age of eighteen it was possible for the *dge-tshul* to take the full vows of the Buddhist monk, pledging himself to the observance of all 253 vows of the code. As such he became a *dge-slong*. A nun was obliged to observe 364 vows. It was, however, open to both monks and nuns to annul their vows and return to the lay life. Otherwise monks could continue their education in more specialised directions with the prospect of becoming at the conclusion of their Tantric studies, abbots (*mkhan-po*) of monasteries not traditionally ruled by an incarnate. There were also different disciplinary, spiritual and liturgical posts inseparable from the character of monastic life. There was some difference between sects in this respect but all had dignitaries and officials who also taught, examined, concerned themselves with general discipline, good behaviour at services and oversaw the provision of tea, soup and the other food served during the services. In the larger monasteries, where the colleges were almost separate organisations, educational, disciplinary and administrative positions were correspondingly numerous. Those that had responsibility for the assets of the monastery might be rich monks appointed for a fixed period. The monasteries were exempt from taxes and the provision of labour and transport, owned land, levied taxes and services from their tenantry and exercised judicial authority over them. Their revenue came also from trade and money-lending and payments made for certain rites performed for layfolk. Private property in a monastery could be held by richer monks who might have their own sources of income from family lands, trade or the private performance of rites. There were also large numbers of lower monks who performed a variety of menial tasks, lighting lamps on altars, the maintenance of buildings, or cooking; a special category of monk recruited from this large body formed a kind of monastic militia (*ldab-ldob*) providing escorts, bodyguards, athletes and police at ceremonies and festivals.

Much of what has been said applied to the larger monasteries which included the great Yellow Hat establishments of Ganden (dGa'-ldan), Se-ra and Drepung ('Bras-spungs) in the neighbourhood of Lhasa. Until the last they were capable of exercising great influence on the management of the country. During the minorities of Dalai Lamas, regents were appointed from certain monasteries and the choice was inevitably influenced by these great houses. At one time their wealth was supplemented by gifts from the Chinese emperor. These three monasteries may have had a population of 20,000 monks between them while Lhasa itself had no more than about 40,000 inhabitants. There were other large monasteries, such as the seat of the Panchen Lama at Tashilhunpo, whose estimated population at the end of the last century was about 4,000 monks. Outside political Tibet lay the great monasteries at sKu-'bum in Qinghai province and at Urga in Mongolia.

The small monasteries were no less important as the grass-roots of the theocracy. They were often intimately connected with the local population, endowed perhaps by prosperous peasants or landowners and drawing their inmates from neighbouring families who built the living quarters for the recruits they regularly provided.

35 *Stupa* of gilt metal. Its
stepped base has an empty
niche formerly containing
an image above it and it is
surmounted by a tapering
spire of thirteen sections
with pennants at the sides
and the sun-moon symbol
of unity at the top. Height
9¾ in. 18th–19th century AD.

STUPAS

A structure closely associated with monasteries but found also as an isolated
monument, in groups, or in miniature as a votive object, is the Indian *stupa*,
known in Tibet as *mchod-rten* (a word sometimes met in a spelling closer to
the pronunciation as 'chörten') (35). Originally it was not an exclusively
Buddhist structure, for its origins went back to the tumulus, or artificial
burial mound found in many early cultures. In India it was used for royal
interments but was soon associated with the Buddhist religion for the
Buddha was said to have commanded that his relics should, after the
traditional burning of his body, be housed in a *stupa*. Their number
increased rapidly with the spread of the religion and some of the most
impressive early Indian monuments are *stupas*. They were considered not
only as fit repositories for the remains of the Buddha himself but also held
objects that he was said to have used and, in addition, commemorated events

in his 'historical' as well as previous legendary lives. *Stupas* were also erected to commemorate other Buddhas and disciples and holy men. They consisted of a solid dome set on a round or rectangular plinth and crowned by a projecting shaft, representing its axis, supporting, as time passed, an increasing number of disks, which originally stood for the parasol emblem of royalty.

The sacred deposits were usually placed in boxes housed in a very small chamber. *Stupas* were worshipped by the rite of circumambulation, which always had to be in a clockwise direction, and offerings were made to it; the construction of a *stupa*, large or small, as well as its maintenance and use as a goal of pilgrimage were amongst the most prominent Buddhist acts of piety and local varieties of the *stupa* are found in all the many countries to which Buddhism has spread.

In Tibet the *stupa* usually consisted of a rectangular base, a number of steps, the ancient dome, now more like an inverted pot with a wider base than mouth, and, crowning it, a tapering finial still modelled to show the disks, whose number had risen to thirteen. There were, however, a number of differences between types of *stupa* and these could go beyond mere detail. There were, for instance, terraced stupas of a polygonal plan with many step-backs. The pilgrim, still following a clockwise progression, ascended from one terrace to the next, on each of which were chapels containing images and wall-paintings, the whole culminating in a shrine at the top. This type was the '*stupa* of many doors'; in central Tibet the most famous was at Gyantse but they were not confined to that region and the same name was given to portable models with niches and inner compartments containing stamped clay plaques, images and paintings which were said to have been carried from village to village by wandering monks for exhibition to the people. Monumental prototypes for the Tibetan terraced *stupa* have been excavated in Bengal and Bihar. Another form of *stupa*, closer to the commoner type already described, differs in having flights of steps on all four sides of the base and leading to the dome. In India an upper processional path so reached was a feature of many *stupas* but in Tibet the space at the foot of the dome was too narrow to be functional. The type of *stupa* with steps was, however, supposed to commemorate one of the eight great events of the Buddha's life, the miraculous descent from the heaven where he had gone to teach his dead mother and the gods his new-found spiritual insights. In another variant of the Tibetan *stupa* the rectangular base was pierced to make a gateway. Such a *stupa* might stand alone or serve as entrance to a town or monastery or at the approach to a bridge. It was through such a *stupa* that the British Mission marched into Lhasa in 1904.

Stupas continued to serve their ancient purpose as reliquaries in Tibet. They contained fragments of bone or the ashes of particularly holy men (cremation was reserved in a country where wood was scarce for persons of sanctity) or objects that had belonged to them, such as clothing; small stamped images or clay plaques, themselves containing relics, were regularly deposited in them as were holy books or parts of them. These objects were not necessarily placed inside the *stupa* at its construction only; many *stupas* had openings into which appropriate objects might continue to be inserted: charms, images, paintings and writings which, being holy but for some reason no longer required, might nevertheless not be thrown away. There were also richly decorated silver and gold *stupas* containing the body of Dalai Lamas in the Potala at Lhasa and of the Panchen Lamas at Tashilhunpo. Smaller model *stupas* were used for ritual purposes, particularly on altars. Amongst these was a type associated with the evangelist Atisa (985–1054), who is commonly represented with a *stupa*. These models were particularly numerous in bKa'-gdams-pa foundations, deriving from Atisa's ministry, and examples five feet high have been quoted.

The symbolic importance of the *stupa* was very great. In early Buddhist India it had stood for the Great Decease, the death of the Buddha, which was the final proof of his conquest over life and death for as a Buddha he was never again to be reborn. In time the *stupa* came to represent Buddhahood itself, the Absolute as pure consciousness or void. The *stupa* also became one of the three supports or receptacles for the threefold division of the sacred into mind, word and body, for Buddhahood was equated with mind; by containing images (body) and books (word) or stamped clay plaques with figures and sacred formulas the *stupa* became a complete Buddhist symbol.

The various parts of the *stupa* also became invested with symbolic meaning and correspondences. Thus the square base was the earth, the circular dome water, the finial with its more or less triangular outline fire as well as the thirteen steps to Enlightenment, the half-moon above it wind and the sun space. Together the last two symbolised the Tantric opposites of the female concept of voidness or knowledge and the male concept of means or compassion united in the ultimate illumination, to which the circle, sometimes a flame, above them corresponded.

WORSHIP AND RITUAL OBJECTS

Altars were found in temples, assembly-halls and monks' cells as well as in private homes and nomad tents. They often consisted of a number of tiers accommodating the objects worshipped and the necessary ritual implements. There was always at least one image; in the temples and assembly-halls of the monasteries some were of considerable size, the central figure

77

36 (left) Brass image of Tara with a painted head and gold-threaded brocade garments consisting of an apron and a 'cloud-collar' with corded edging. Height 6 in. 17th–18th century AD.

37 (right) Silver butter lamp on a stand decorated with lotus petals; its stem consists of the vase of immortality. Height 6 in. 19th–20th century AD.

being that of the deity to whom the temple was dedicated or the patron or founder of the order to which the monastery belonged; sometimes there were three principal figures, depending on the sect. Beside or below them could be smaller images. All images might be draped with scarves as offerings and clothed with aprons and collars (36); some ritual accessories were also provided with 'garments' (42). In front of the images were normally seven

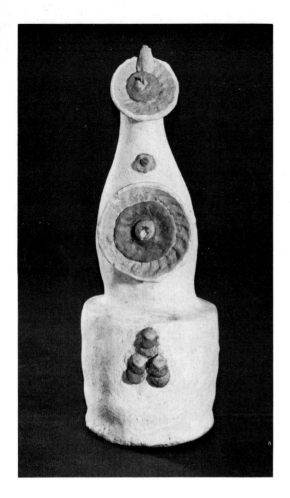

38 (left) Offering cake (*gtor-ma*), usually made of *rtsam-pa*, butter and sugar with coloured discs of butter on the front but sometimes, as here, made of painted clay for economy. Height 7¾ in. 19th century AD.

39 (right) Censer with a suspension chain and an openwork lid with dragon motif. The brass body carries an applied decorative register in copper. Censers of this kind were carried in procession and at sacred dances. Height without chain 11 in. 19th century AD.

shallow bowls containing water which was changed every morning by the temple-keeper, who at the same time lit lamps, burned incense and offered short prayers. At least one lamp was constantly kept alight on a Tibetan altar (37). There were often more lamps, usually in the form of pedestal bowls with a small hole in the bottom to receive the cotton wick. The bowl was filled with butter which solidified, acting like candle wax. Lighting a butter lamp or adding fresh butter were common acts of piety. The shallow bowls served for the offerings that accompanied rites; they are variously called the essential, homage or drawing-near offerings. While water alone sufficed in routine circumstances, for special ceremonies the offerings were made in kind and consisted of the gifts traditionally offered to a guest: water for drinking and washing, flowers, incense, lamps, perfume (in the form of saffron water for anointing) and food. The flowers and incense were placed in the bowls stuck into rice or *rtsam-pa*; the flowers might be reduced to a single paper imitation and the incense took the form of joss-sticks made of juniper or sandalwood powdered and mixed with musk and clay.

The food was usually a *gtor-ma*, a cake made of *rtsam-pa* and butter, coloured and with disks and other devices stuck on the front (38). *gTor-mas* varied greatly depending on the rite. A painted dummy, supported on a tripod, was sometimes used as an economical substitute. These offerings were accompanied by the recitation of hymns and the sounding of various instruments and constituted 'external worship'; the rite of 'internal worship', or the worshipper's offering of himself represented through the five senses, used other cult utensils: sight was symbolised by a mirror, a polished metal disk on a stand; sound by small cymbals or a bell; a shell with perfumes or incense sticks stood for smell; a cake or other food represented taste, while touch was indicated by a piece of silk. A page of text, representing mind, was added to the original group of five. Other objects appearing on an altar were a miniature *stupa* or *mchod-rten*, the ancient Buddhist reliquary, and a book. Together with the image they represented the three supports already mentioned: the reliquary corresponded to buddhahood or the spiritual plane, the book symbolised the verbal plane and the Buddhist doctrine in particular, while the image (or painting) represented the physical plane and monkhood. This group of three objects, which must be present during worship, was thus equated with the ancient Buddhist profession of faith with which the believer, proclaiming his recourse to the Three Refuges or Supports of the Buddha, the Doctrine and its representatives, the monks, performed the essential act that made him a Buddhist. Incense burners (39) also formed part of the usual altar equipment and were kept on a lower shelf; musical instruments were also kept on or beside altars; a water jug for filling the smaller vessels stood nearby as did a dish for offerings of rice, flower vases and a rice *mandala*, i.e., a tiered circular object representing the universe which was made up daily to symbolise the offering up of the world. *Gahus* or talisman boxes were also kept on altars (40).

Many other objects were used in more specialised rituals required in Tantric worship and could have magical as well as mystical application. An important distinction was that between utensils used in the cult of tranquil and fierce divinities. Thus for the fierce form of deity there was also a set of

40 Talisman box (*gahu*) with attachment lugs. The silver front, fitting over a copper box, has a window to show an image or plaque inside and is embossed with scrolling and Buddhist symbols. 6 × 5½ × 2 in. 19th–20th century AD.

offerings but the incense was interpreted as human fat, the butter in the lamp corresponded to decomposing human flesh, water was replaced with bile and food represented flesh and bones in the form of a *gtor-ma* modelled to show human features.

A separate room in the temples, called *mgon-khang*, was given over to the worship of the fierce protector deities, both of the general kind and those more specifically local, the aboriginal deities taken over by Buddhism as custodians of the temple now standing in the place that had, in popular belief, once belonged to them. Considered especially holy, the *mgon-khang* was normally closed to strangers and always to women and married men. The doors are described as low and narrow and carved with monstrous faces and the light within was feeble. At the entrance animals stuffed with straw hung from the ceiling; these animals were said to be the messengers of the protectors. Here, too, were collections of arms and armour. Traditional weapons and armour were of the same kind as worn by the protectors in paintings, images and textual descriptions. From their long use in warfare

these and sometimes more modern fire-arms were thought to have acquired magic properties and thus to have become suitable for presentation to the fierce protectors. They were also explained as trophies won from enemies and brigands – of which Tibet had a large number – who had been killed by the favour of the protector gods. In these rooms masks for the dance festivals were also stored (pl. 10).

These shrines had their own kind of wall and cloth-paintings, usually with a black background, and the terrifying figures depicted on them were surrounded by red flames (41). The images, as in the main temple, were draped with scarves and in worship a flat drum hung in a frame was beaten with a muffled stick. Butter lamps were also kept burning in these shrines. There were monks who chose to spend their lives in these rooms, realising in themselves the essential unity that was believed to link the terrors and forces of the dark side of personality with the peaceful realisations of conscious serenity. For as the temple was considered a projection of the universe, so within it was found a place for perils and evil which were overcome by the terrible and warlike aspects of a merciful deity.

The following descriptions will treat ritual objects without describing complete ceremonies. Many were widely used. Perhaps the most important are the thunderbolt symbol (*vajra*) and bell (*ghanta*) which were often kept on altars, particularly in the monk's cells and used at communal ceremonies. The *vajra* was held in the right hand and the bell in the left and both were moved in formal gestures during recitation and reading. The *vajra,* as has already been explained, represents on its own the adamantine or unbreakable and unchanging essence of Buddhahood which can be defined as 'total void'; in conjunction with the bell, however, it represented one of the joint factors in the quest for liberation, the male principle of compassion as the means, while the bell was the female principle of wisdom or knowledge of the voidness of all things.

As well as symbolising sight in the ritual of 'internal worship' the mirror on a stand had other functions. It was placed on altars in front of an image or painting so as to reflect it and thus signify that all things including the sacred images are reflexes of the imagination; in one ritual holy water from a jug was poured over it. The water received added sanctity from this indirect contact with an already sacred object and was then caught in a chalice, in bowls or in the worshipper's cupped hands. Instead of a mirror on a stand a small mirror, hung from the spout of the jug and pointed towards the image, performed the same function. The mirror also drove away evil spirits who could not bear to see themselves in it. Holy water in the jug was mixed with saffron and sugar. It formed part of the eight offerings but when sprinkled a stopper-rod, placed in the jug and surmounted by sacred *kusa* grass and peacock feathers, was used (42).

83

41 *Thang-ka* of the dGe-lugs-pa sect showing the four-armed protector Mahakala holding a chopper, sword, trident and blood-filled skull cup, seated below the *siddha* Saraha and accompanied by two skeleton spirits, the protectress Lha-mo and four bird-headed fierce goddesses. 34 × 22 in. 18th–19th century AD.

42 (left) Holy water vase with a silk brocade and cotton 'garment' and a stopper rod surmounted with peacock feathers. Silver, partly gilt. Height with feathers 16 in. 19th century AD.

43 (right) Skull cup consisting of a human skull top set in metal with ornamented metal cover and triangular pedestal. Height 8 in. 19th–20th century AD.

Rituals also used a mounted and covered skull cup (43). This type of bowl was often made of a genuine skull or could be a metal version. In one ritual context where two such bowls were used one held perfumed medicinal herbs or the five kinds of ambrosia while the other was filled with substitutes for blood and the five kinds of flesh (the cosmic significance of the number will already have been noted); another ceremony also provided for two skull cups containing beer and tea, standing respectively for ambrosia and blood. In

84

44 (left) Silver libation bowl on a stand. Medallions around the bowl contain Buddhist auspicious symbols; the stand is ringed with small applied lotus petals and skulls. Height 9 in. 19th century AD.

45 (right) Painted wooden vase of life with four leaves hanging from the rim; a plaque inserted into the top shows Amitayus, the Dhyani Buddha of Longevity. Perhaps from an image or used in ritual. Height 10½ in. 19th century AD.

ceremonies connected with the fierce protector deities real blood was prescribed. The use of articles of bone was held to symbolise the transitoriness of human life, although a skull cup of beer representing the wine of life was used in a ceremony for longevity. An unmounted skull cup, such as deities often carry, was used by yogins outside monasteries. Other vessels included a form of libation jug of Chinese style used for an offering of tea, beer and milk; this was poured into a bowl on a stand (44) which stood on a

85

dish and contained a similar mixture with seeds. Another ritual object is a covered, often fluted, dish to hold rice or barley which was scattered in offering to spirits.

A small and portable vase of life, the attribute which the Tathagata or Dhyani Buddha Amitayus, the Buddha of Eternal Life, holds in his lap (45), was used in ceremonies for longevity. On the birth of a child Amitayus is invoked by a lama with a bell and hand-drum; when he is believed to have entered the vase, it is placed on the head of parents and child. A more elaborate ceremony requiring the use of a vase of life has been described at length by Waddell as the Eucharist of Lamaism. The celebrant identifies himself with Amitayus and in the course of a long ritual he takes the vase from the altar and places it on the heads of the kneeling worshippers reciting the spell of Amitayus, which, like so many Tibetan invocations, is derived from the Indian sacred language, Sanskrit.

A number of objects belong to a doubtful category, for in the present uncertain state of knowledge of the history of Tibetan ritual it is not clear whether they are ritual implements or detachable attributes from larger images. It can be argued that such objects are ritual if they are used by the Tantric worshipper to identify himself with a particular deity; weapons are indeed carried by mediums when they go into an oracular trance and are possessed by the god whose attributes they are holding. To offer weapons to a protector deity will serve to strengthen him as a defender of the faith. A number of collections possess the curved chopper surmounted by the thunderbolt prongs (*karttrika*) which one authority quotes as being used to cut the life roots of enemies and obstacle-creating demons. Such choppers are extremely common attributes of fierce deities, often held in the opposite hand to the skull cup. Another attribute carried by many deities, which may have had a ritual application is the *khatvanga,* sometimes explained as a magician's wand (46).

The British Museum's collection has a sumptuously worked example which bears a Chinese reign-mark (AD 1403–24). A *khatvanga* consists of a long wand surmounted by the vase of life, a freshly severed head, a decomposing head, a skull and a pronged thunderbolt symbol. Passages in Tantric texts can be read to mean that in the course of his practice the yogin carried the *khatvanga* when identifying himself with the central deity of the ritual.

Moving nearer to popular religion and magic one may mention the various forms of prayer-wheel. These consist of cylinders containing tightly rolled texts or repeated invocations, usually blockprinted, which are revolved from right to left so that the texts, if visible, could be read. Some prayer-wheels do, indeed, have short invocations on the outside. Prayer-wheels range from huge barrels for which heights of thirty to forty feet and diameters of fifteen

86

46 Steel *khatvanga*, an attribute of many deities and of Padmasambhava. Inlaid with gold and silver. Length 17 in. Reign-mark of the Yongle emperor (AD 1403–24).

to twenty feet have been quoted to the common and hand-held cylinder turned on a stick. Their importance derives from the Indian Tantric development in Buddhism that emphasised the power of sound, whether as a mystic formula (*mantra*) or as syllables with which a deity was especially associated. Smaller prayer-barrels are found along monastery walls, inside the porticoes of temples, in the open where they are turned by the wind and water or in miniature indoor shrines and turned by hand. The hand-held prayer-wheel (47), most commonly of metal and used everywhere in the Lamaist world, revolves on a pin stuck loosely into a handle, with a ring of shell or ivory between cylinder and handle. A heavy cube or ball, usually of metal, attached to the side of the cylinder by a chain or cord sets up a centrifugal momentum which turns the cylinder on its axis. The commonest formula in a prayer-wheel is said to be the six-syllable invocation to Avalokitesvara (*Om mani-padme hum*) and from a published calculation based on a prayer-wheel containing 100 pages of this invocation printed 400 times on a page, it follows that a single revolution of that wheel would be the equivalent – to the Tibetan – of repeating the formula 40,000 times.

47 Hand-held prayer-wheel. A silver cylinder, containing blockprinted prayers and ornamented with scrolling, lotus petals and red and green stones. Secured with a pin on a wooden handle bound in brass. Length 9½ in. 19th–20th century AD.

RELIGIOUS MUSIC AND INSTRUMENTS

More than one author has described the unearthly effect of the chanting and instrumental music of Tibetan ritual. The effect is produced with a minimum of means: the human voice, droning or chanting in low registers, progressing by semi- and quarter-tones, and a small number of wind and percussion instruments – cymbals, bells, shawms, trumpets and drums – which made up the temple orchestra, but also had separate functions. The wind instruments were normally blown in pairs so that the sound should not be interrupted by a player's need to draw breath; the player was trained to breathe through the nose. Cymbals of course also came in pairs though a small cymbal with clapper was also known. Tibetans had devised a form of musical notation consisting of wavy lines of varying thickness which accompanied the text to be chanted. These lines indicated when the voice should rise, swell and fall in relation to the words chanted; the sounding of instruments was shown pictorially by, for example, a figure of a shell or drumstick at the appropriate place.

There were three kinds of cymbals, two large and one small. The larger were distinguished according to the size of the central boss. Those with small bosses were used for the worship of peaceful deities and were essential for all offering rituals and certain Tantric ceremonies. They were struck gently and held vertically. Cymbals with large central bosses were used in the worship of fierce deities; they were held horizontally and struck with some force. They not only formed part of the orchestra but gave the signal at the beginning or end of a chant or service. The small cymbals were used by monks in their private devotions, in the ritual for the spirit of the dead hovering between its last state and the next (*bar-do*) and to summon hungry spirits to accept offerings.

They were also used to represent sound, as part of the eight offerings, and hearing in the offering of the five senses and their objects. Cymbals were made of bell metal, a true bronze or alloy of copper and tin in varying proportions to achieve the tone required.

Wind instruments included trumpets made of conch, metal and bone as well as a form of oboe or shawm (pl. 8). The latter instrument was usually of wood with metal bell and other parts, but sometimes entirely of metal; it had seven holes on the upper side and an eighth at the back for the thumb. This, the only instrument of the religious orchestra capable of providing a melody, performed the highest part in the ensemble and was used for all ceremonies except exorcism. The metal covering allowed considerable ornament and a pair in the British Museum covered in silver is richly set with coloured stones in the Nepalese style. The trumpets were a series of natural trumpets of different sizes of which the largest, a long telescopic instrument in three

48 Telescope trumpet in three sections, here shown retracted. Hammered and brazed copper with riveted brass decoration, partly silvered, with two suspension rings and a silver wishing jewel emblem.
Length 33 in.
19th–20th century AD.

sections, could extend for as much as sixteen feet, producing a pro-portionately deep tone. They were made of strips of beaten metal, brazed along their length and ringed at the edges of their sections with applied ornamentation in contrasting metal (48). They had various uses: in the temple orchestra they provided a low drone in contrast to the shawms; they

49 Two musicians of a rNying-ma-pa monastery wearing wigs and playing shawms.
(Photo H. E. Richardson)

were used in higher Tantric ceremonies but not, in the liturgy of a number of
schools, to accompany hymns. They announced the beginning of ceremonies, on occasion from the roofs of monasteries, and were used during the
religious dances. They might be supported only on the ground, held up by
other monks or placed on special stands. Like the other wind instruments
they were used in pairs. Smaller pairs of metal trumpets, either straight or
curved, were also used in the temples and at religious dance ceremonies.
Their bells sometimes took the form of a dragon's head and might have
textile ornaments attached to them.

Yet another form of trumpet was made of a human thigh-bone covered
with skin or ornamented with various metal settings and bound with wire. It
appears as the attribute of fierce deities and was used in a variety of

ceremonies connected with them and especially for exorcism. This type of trumpet was held capable of subduing gods and demons. Traditionally the best bones were obtained from Brahmins, and especially a sixteen year old Brahmin girl, but almost any source was acceptable, including victims of accident, disease and murder. Trumpets of tiger's thigh-bone are also mentioned. Conch shells provided another form of trumpet with metal mouthpiece and textile pendant, or more or less elaborately mounted in a metal panel or flange with a tube to prolong the valve and thus deepen and amplify the sound. They were used to summon monks to prayer and ritual ablutions and were part of the monastic orchestra; in eastern Tibet it is said that they were used for ceremonies to avert the hail which was a constant threat to ripening crops.

Drums were of various kinds. One, the *damaru,* was inherited from India; it appears, for instance, as an attribute of deities in both Hindu and Buddhist sculpture. It took the form of two hemispheres connected by their domes

50 Skull drum (*damaru*) consisting of two skull tops covered in skin, with a handle and clappers of leather. Height 4¼ in. 19th century AD.

51 Wooden cymbal box covered in lacquered canvas, with brass mounts and openwork medallions containing floral decoration. Height 9 in; diameter 13¾ in. 19th century AD.

like a squat hour-glass. A cord or strap of textile or leather at the join projected to form a handle. Also attached to the strap on opposite sides of the 'waist' were cords ending in small leather balls or knobs which struck the surface of the drum alternately as it was jerked from side to side. The drum could be made of wood, painted with designs, or two skull tops (50), closed with skin and provided with an ornamental silk pendant. Such drums had many uses. They marked intervals in recitation, drew the attention, with other instruments, of the gods being invoked and induced a suitable state of mind in the exorcist during the recitation of his spells. The *damaru* was ritually paired with the bone trumpet and, with the bell, was used for rain-making. The sources of the skull tops were again various: children who had died at the age of eight or were born of an incestuous union were thought to possess special magical power and the victim of a violent death was also considered suitable. This type of drum was also a frequent attribute of Tibetan deities.

A somewhat larger convex-sided wooden drum supported on a pole and hence called a pole drum was used in various ceremonies inside temples and in procession. It was struck with a long curved stick, shaped a little like a question mark, with a textile or leather ball at the end. A drum suspended from a frame after the Chinese fashion was beaten on a balcony or rooftop when monks were to be summoned to an assembly, in ceremonies involving all monks and during the most important Tantric ceremonies. They have already been mentioned as occurring in the protectors' shrines. The hand-bell, the regular companion of the thunderbolt symbol, was also used together with the hand-drum (*damaru*) or thigh-bone trumpet in exorcistic ceremonies. Like the thunderbolt symbol and hand-bell, musical instruments were also carried in special cases. The British Museum's collection has several examples, including a crude wooden box for trumpets in which the space they occupy has been hollowed out, a cylindrical woollen carrier for a wooden hand-drum and a large and handsome wooden box, painted red and bound with decorative metal straps, for a pair of cymbals used in ceremonies devoted to the fierce deities (51).

DANCES

A colourful, emotional and complex ceremony through which the monasteries indirectly associated layfolk, who were not admitted to monastic services, with the rites and meditations of Tibetan Buddhism is the mystery play (*lha-'cham*), the most famous of which was performed by monks in front of their monasteries at the year's end. It appears to have absorbed ancient concepts of human sacrifice which, as part of the earlier religion of Tibet, is known to have been practised in the time of the central monarchy. The play, which lasted two days and was a sequence of mimed and mainly masked dances, centred on a human effigy of dough, paper or hide. This sacrificial model, provided with a soul and entrails in a previous ceremony, was attacked and the evil it contained destroyed and what good it possessed sent to a paradise. Thus the ceremony involved exorcism so that the new year could start freshly purged.

The participants consisted of two groups, the Tantric officiants, who wore tall tapering hats and were called black hat dancers, and the masked actors; among these were the god of death, represented as Yama with a horned bull's head, or as Mahakala, burning-ground spirits (*citipati*), who appeared as skeletons with skull masks (52), and other beings such as the stags who participated in the dismemberment of the sacrificial victim. Many of the actors wore rich garments of Chinese silk and the masks were made of layers of cloth and paper mixed with glue and brightly painted. The number of participants, especially at the greater monasteries, was very large and the variety of masks represents the development of the ceremony by the absorption of stories of the history and triumphs of Buddhism. One such theme is the assassination of Glang-dar-ma (842), the last of the early kings

52 Painted paper and canvas skull mask with black nose and mouth; other features are shown in red. The mask also has multi-coloured pleated attachments. Worn in the New Year dance by monks dressed entirely to look like skeletons. Width about 23 in. 19th century AD.

and a persecutor of Buddhism; comic relief was provided by masked figures representing the early Indian teachers, whose foreign appearance was turned to ridicule, and by a Chinese monk of the defeated side when Indian and Chinese Buddhism contended for supremacy in Tibet (about 790). As the dancers included protectors of the religion and their entourage, who had already, as part of the New Year ceremony, been worshipped by the monks, deities of the liturgy were shown to the people in a form rooted in ancient belief, for masks, once venerated as representing protectors, seem to have possessed magical properties enabling these deities to manifest themselves. In this connection it becomes natural that the dances should have been performed according to a precise ritual to the sound of drums, shawms and trumpets, all instruments connected with worship. The full meaning of the *'cham* may not always have been understood but it attracted the keen attention of the lay spectators who came in large numbers, pitching their tents near the monasteries if their homes lay far enough away.

Another popular form of drama was that provided by strolling players called, after one of the characters represented, *a-che-lha-mo* or 'lady-

94

goddess'. It, too, had a religious character insofar as the theme comprised *jatakas,* or stories of the historical Buddha's supposed previous lives, and tales of past heroes or heroines renowned for their piety and miracles. In these dramas were worn masks called 'hunter's' masks, more or less triangular, flat, edged with hair and made of wool or felt (53). Amongst those that wore them were buffoons and narrators but the term 'hunter' appears to derive originally from an incarnation of a bodhisattva who, as fisherman in an ancient story, captured a fairy, the 'lady-goddess' after whom the drama form was named. Unlike the *lha-'cham* this form of drama could have actresses who wore colourful garments (pl. 4) and some troupes performed before the Dalai Lama.

53 'Hunter's' mask, worn by actors in strolling troupes, made of wool with applied features in satin, a goat's hair fringe and shell ear-rings. Height 25 in. 19th century AD.

4
Arts and Crafts

With examples of painting, metal sculpture, ritual and other sacred objects, textiles and items of everyday use the material culture of Tibet, despite the remoteness and long isolation of the country, is surprisingly well represented in foreign collections. Although there have been some pioneering and specialised studies, the Tibetan arts and crafts have never been sufficiently investigated for reasons already mentioned in the introduction and their history remains to be written.

There is general agreement that influences from outside the country were decisive in shaping its arts and crafts. Craftsmen were employed within Tibet for secular and religious purposes perhaps from a very early period and certainly from the time that the central monarchy was established under Srong-brtsan-sgam-po (627–650). The Chinese chroniclers of the Tang dynasty (618–907) refer to the skill of Tibetans in metalworking – an allusion not so much to their weapons as their ability to work gold – and indicate also that the traditional Tibetan flat-roofed style of building was already in existence. During the age of the central monarchy temples were built, paintings are said to have been executed in the cathedral (Jo-khang) at Lhasa and images are also referred to. Large statues in the round, representing Srong-brtsan-sgam-po and his two wives, in both Jo-khang and the Potala are quite unlike anything else known in Tibet but, since they are heavily painted and clothed it is difficult to judge their age and style and they may indeed not be contemporary. There is some evidence of Chinese influence on the way of life of the aristocracy at this early time and the solitary stone lion carved in the round on a ninth-century royal tomb may be a provincial Chinese production, although Persian influence has also been suggested. The first monastery, at bSam-yas (10), built about AD 779, is said to have been in imitation of a celebrated Indian foundation, Uddandapura, which, however, no longer exists for comparison. Tradition further maintains that three styles were employed at bSam-yas: Tibetan, Chinese and Indian; a castle near by had a Tibetan ground floor, a first floor in the style of Khotan

96

7 Monk dancer's silk dress. The damask bodice is covered in floral patterns and Buddhist symbols and the sleeves and skirt are mainly brocade and decorated with dragons, clouds, landscape and jewellery motifs. Height 57 in. 19th century AD.

8 Shawm made of silver over a wooden body. It is richly decorated with scrollwork, gilding and precious stones. The two birds on the bell are set with turquoise, lapis, shell and rubies. Length 24 in. 19th century AD.

9 Jade tea-cup on a silver stand. Incised flowers and scrolling decorate the stand and the silver cover. A coral bead is fixed on top of the cover by a pin with a flower-shaped head. Height 5⅛ in. 19th century AD.

10 Painted clay and canvas mask of a monk dancer. Height 10 in. Said to be from Ladakh, 19th century AD.

11 *Thang-ka* showing the four-headed, twelve-armed tutelary deity Samvara and his 'wisdom partner'. His attributes include an elephant skin, a wand, a chopper, a skull cup and a drum. The other figures shown include, above, Vairocana (left), the historical Buddha (centre) and the future Buddha (right), and below, the Buddha of long life (centre). 51 × 30½ in. 18th century AD.

12 *Thang-ka* showing Saraha, an Indian *siddha*, holding the arrow of comprehension. He appears with other *siddhas* and, above, his pupil Nagarjuna (left), and the scholar Bu-ston (1290–1364), holding an oblong book (right). 32 × 23 in. 18–19th century AD.

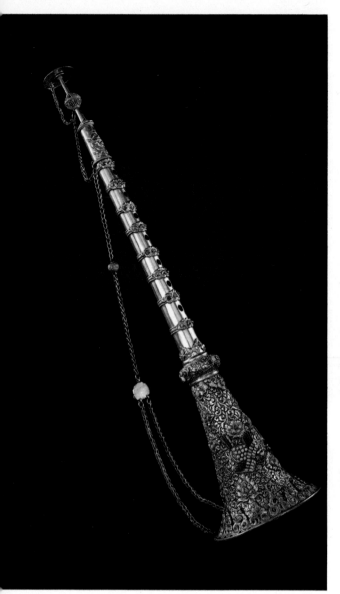

8

9

in Central Asia, a second in Chinese style and a third in the Indian manner, with craftsmen of each of the countries responsible for the work. Although these traditions cannot now be verified (they may for instance refer to wall-paintings or images), the combination tells us what influences went into the creation of Tibetan monuments and nearly all its arts and crafts. The Indian style would no doubt have been from Bihar and Bengal and closely related to the Nepalese which, though already present earlier, would increasingly have replaced the eastern Indian source after 1200. The survival of eastern Indian bronzes recorded in and from Tibet, will have served as models for a considerable time afterwards. Nepalese inspiration was then and later of capital importance. Kashmiri and related styles were established in the western Himalayas owing to the important part played by the kingdom of Gu-ge in the revival of Buddhism in the tenth century and its dependence on Kashmiri Buddhists. But after the rise of a Muslim dynasty in Kashmir in 1337 a distinctive western Tibetan style, though it persisted perhaps for some centuries, became increasingly provincial.

Chinese influence, though subject to fluctuation, has never ceased to make itself felt in sculpture, painting, architecture and the minor arts and crafts since the time of the Yuan dynasty (1279–1368), when Tibetan Buddhists acquired a powerful influence over the Mongol Emperor of China, Kublai Khan (1260–94). A Sino-Tibetan art developed, expressing itself in blockprints, paintings and bronzes, which in varying degrees combined Chinese elements with Nepalese and related Tibetan idioms. Paintings and images of the Ming period (1368–1644) form the largest group of dated Lamaistic objects (54) and must have exercised some influence, for

54 Gilt brass figure of four-handed Manjusri, Bodhisattva of Wisdom, holding his sword, a bow and the stalk of the lotus supporting the book of knowledge. Height 7 in. Peking, reign-mark of the Yongle emperor (AD 1403–1424).

97

they are known to have been executed as Imperial gifts to powerful monasteries. The political ascendancy of China in Tibet from the eighteenth century renewed the artistic impact. Under the Qing (1644–1911) gifts were made to monasteries, and Manchu emperors, particularly Qianlong (1736–96), were Lamaist Buddhists and had temples built for which many images were made. From the seventeenth century the Mongols as a people had also become Buddhists and images from the Mongol region appear strongly Sino-Tibetan. Painting in particular underwent strong Chinese influence in the final period of Tibetan art.

Throughout this time the Newar artists and craftsmen of Nepal were active; many were settled in Tibet and must have had Tibetan followers. Their influence is evident in a number of early and datable buildings with murals and statuary. There was a great output in sculpture, ritual, decorative and utilitarian craftsmanship in wood, metal, clay and papier-mâché and there is every reason to suppose that it was executed in Tibet even when the manner may have been foreign. A late eighteenth-century Chinese account of the country claims that 'Tibetan carpenters and stone cutters are very expert. The artisans make also gold, silver, copper, tin and filagree vessels set with pearls ... the work being as good as Chinese. They carve very finely men, different objects and bunches of flowers reproducing very exactly the originals'. Since Nepalese images and paintings sometimes have dated dedications it is possible to support datings of similar objects thought to have been produced in Tibet.

It is clear, however, that when Chinese and Nepalese styles are left out of account there is still a range of varied material which cannot be dated securely. The art is usually anonymous and never absolutely dated; artists travelled from one monastery to another and, as the objects were often portable, they will also have travelled and been imitated. Some artists and styles are named in Tibetan inscriptions and literature; the latter discusses stylistic origins and the alloys that were used for metalwork. But it is not usually possible to connect these classifications with the material at our disposal. The dating of most Tibetan art remains subjective and hazardous. In 1969 P. Pal's exhibition catalogue *The Art of Tibet* was prefaced by the statement: 'since Tibet's art is largely anonymous and undated the chronology suggested here is tentative ...'; in 1977 the catalogue of the great exhibition of Lamaist art held in Paris and Munich also began by admitting that 'the proposed dates are all hypothetical; in the present state of our knowledge no great accuracy is possible in this respect'. The position today is unchanged.

PAINTING

Tibetan painting is known abroad largely from the scroll-paintings, sometimes called banners and often by different spellings of their Tibetan name, *thang-ka*. They are easily carried when rolled up, unlike mural painting, which was very widespread in monasteries, temples, palaces, private homes, forts and halls but is almost unrepresented outside Tibet. Paint was also applied to images and clay plaques, to buildings in vertical and horizontal stripes, to architectural features like window surrounds and on wooden pillars, beams and brackets and on ceilings inside buildings. Although the existence of wall-paintings has been well known, adequate colour photographs are only now being published, principally of interiors in Ladakh and Bhutan outside political Tibet. Painting, an important Indian inheritance, was also used to illuminate manuscripts and to decorate the traditional wooden covers which enclosed them (pl. 2).

Wall painting seems to go back to the beginnings of Buddhist art. Those in the rock-cut monasteries of Ajanta in western India are well known, and the earliest paintings may antedate the Christian era; some painting survives from the artistic province of Gandhara, mainly from Afghanistan (*c.* fifth century AD), and from there influences reached out to the Buddhist establishments in Central Asia along the trade-route to China; the murals at Dunhuang are well known to all students of Buddhist art. Recent excavation at the great monastic university site of Nalanda has revealed paintings in a shrine that may be earlier than the tenth century. Nalanda was a major source with other Indian monasteries of influence on Tibetan culture.

The subject-matter of Tibetan monastery wall painting was often a highly complex rendering of Tantric cycles, consisting of the principal god of the texts acknowledged as authoritative in the monastery, with his manifestations, entourage and protectors. To prepare the surface for wall-paintings a thick plaster of earth mixed with finely chopped straw was applied, carefully smoothed and sized. The paint was of the strong and crude variety also used on architectural elements and furniture. The wall-paintings that have been studied for art history and iconography comprise the work, much of it early, in the temples and monasteries of western Tibet, including Ladakh, and that found in temples and monasteries in south-central Tibet. One of these, the stepped *stupa*-temple at Gyantse, the famous sKu-'bum, consisted of 73 chapels said to contain 27,529 painted images.

The scroll-paintings, which are well represented in foreign collections, derive from the Indian tradition of painting on cloth, no examples of which survive, though there are many references in literature. The closest approximation to these lost models occurs perhaps in some surviving examples of paintings on cloth from Nepal or in Nepalese style which also

99

resemble ancient and sometimes dated Indian paintings on manuscripts and wooden book covers, some of which have been preserved in Nepal. As in the case of early Indian manuscripts it remains possible that the Tibetan temples will still yield ancient paintings exported from India before or at the time of the destruction of its Buddhist shrines.

Thang-kas in their developed form were paintings entirely framed in silk on cloth which is usually a loosely woven cotton; canvas is rare but silk is found, especially in China and sometimes even leather and skin were used. The widespread use of cotton is reflected in two of the Tibetan words for paintings used in addition to *thang-ka*, i.e. *ras-bris* and *ras-ri-mo*, where *ras* means 'cotton'. Usually in one piece but sometimes with another sewn on, damp cotton was stretched over a wooden frame, to which it was stitched before being treated with a paste of lime or chalk mixed with a gum obtained from animal hide. Repeated rubbing of the surface with some well-polished object, such as a stone or shell, eliminated porousness. The drawing started with the central image; the other figures and features were added later. Charcoal was commonly used to produce the outline, which was done free-hand or by using a grid to ensure the correctness of the important traditional canon of proportions: the different parts of the body were fixed fractions of the whole. Another system depended on the pounce, or spray pattern, which consists of a drawing or printed figure on paper with holes pricked at intervals through which the charcoal is sifted, sprayed or pressed to produce a dotted pattern. Ink was used to go over the charcoal outline or join the dots produced from the pounce. The outlines were also printed from woodblocks or metal plates.

The artist did not necessarily prepare the canvas and draw the outline himself. This was left to an apprentice, while the finer work and the application of gold were done by the master painter. Both monks and laymen could be involved in the work. A monk would direct the production of complex compositions, especially when they depended on knowledge of texts. Painting was done with brushes made of twigs with hollowed ends to hold animal hairs; sometimes the hair was simply bound to the stick. Paints were produced from earths, minerals and vegetable substances, though in recent times foreign chemical paints have been used. The traditional substances were ground and mixed with water, glue and chalk; the presence of glue produced a stronger bond but the paints remain easily soluble so that a *thang-ka* is readily damaged by damp. The paints were applied in a specific order and particular details were executed on astrologically favourable days; delicate work and the application of gold were left to the end.

Colour schemes provide a native classification of the paintings. Probably the most common group has the largest variety of colours. Another uses a uniform ground either of gold paint or red vermilion with outlines in a

55 The Potala at Lhasa with the festive display of giant appliqué embroidered '*thang-kas*'. (Photo H. E. Richardson)

contrasting colour. The same technique can be used with a black ground. Sometimes these grounds are enlivened by a limited range of colours in the execution of the figures, a device which can be particularly striking when the contrasts are achieved against black. The variety of the first group was, moreover, repeated in silk either with hand embroidery and weaving techniques or appliqué work, sewn or glued. Such *thang-kas* can produce particularly impressive effects. They were sometimes huge and were hung on special occasions from monastery walls (55).

The finished painting was surrounded with a silk or brocade border. Formerly plain pieces of cloth were attached to the tops and bottoms of the painting with staves above and below for suspension and stretching respectively. The lower stave was made heavier by wooden or metal knobs at each end. The practice of framing the painting entirely in silk was Chinese in origin but, while Chinese and Japanese mounts were pasted to the painting, in Tibet the surround was sewn on. Immediately framing the painting were two thin bands of red and yellow known as the rainbow, symbolising the radiance from the sacred surface. The upper portion of the silk mount was shorter than the lower, into which a rectangular inset was fitted. This symbolised the spiritual 'doorway' into the picture. The entire surface of painting and mount was covered by a dust-curtain which sometimes consisted of a number of different coloured strips. Two strips of silk hung in front of the dust-cover and these may remain suspended in front of the painting when the cover is gathered up through a cord at the top of the mount. Attached to the top was also a pair of threads or leather strips to hang the painting or tie it together when rolled. The back of the painting may also be lined but usually the cloth was left accessible, for there may be inscriptions ranging from – very rare – dates, names of donors, pious formulas and prayers to mystic syllables and the hand- or footprints, always in pairs, of the consecrating lama. Not only was a painting, like any image, consecrated by various rites; the artist had also to purify himself before and during the work. A lama blessed his atelier and implements and in certain instances the artist had to be an initiate of the religious tradition for which he was working.

The subject-matter of the paintings was entirely religious and covered a wide range of forms and intentions. Many paintings were devotional: sacred pictures inducing good thoughts, illustrating good examples and helping to accumulate merit. Painting could also be meditational, serving to illustrate theological positions, to concentrate the mind and train its power ultimately to project the image of the deity and its entourage, conceived as arising out of the void, without recourse to visual aids. In this group are paintings of the Buddhas, bodhisattvas, tutelary and guardian deities variously disposed. A more complete category of meditational painting is represented by the geometric *mandala* (18), for it embodied very specific prescriptions for a complex programme of meditation and the realisation of unity with the Absolute. Another specialised category is connected with the Tibetan conception of the intermediate state between death and rebirth (*bar-do*), a response to the Buddhist doctrine of transmigration and the terrors it provoked if the possibility of unfavourable retribution could not be set aside. The *bar-do mandala* or sets of *mandalas* illustrated peaceful and wrathful deities, all of them emanations of Samantabhadra as the Supreme Buddha, which appeared to the dead person in a given sequence within a period of forty-nine days between his death and rebirth or liberation. Acquaintance with the *bar-do* doctrine and the manifestations to be experienced during it together with readings from the texts during at least part of the period were held to assist the deceased to recognise the apparitions at their true symbolic worth and procure him liberation.

A more generally doctrinal type of painting is the 'Wheel of Life' which occurs both as a *thang-ka* and on painted walls in the entrance to temples. It consists of a compartmented wheel held by a demonic figure representing

102

56 Lama seated on a high-backed chair with flanking lamas and monks and a table of ritual implements before him. Appliqué embroidery. 43 × 30½ in. Bhutan, 19th century AD.

the impermanence which Buddhism assigns to all manifestations of the phenomenal world. Within the wheel are six segments representing the superior and inferior worlds in which one may be reborn; in the rim are small scenes symbolising the twelve stages of the causal progression by which reincarnation takes place and in the hub are three animals symbolic of lust (cock), anger (snake) and ignorance (pig).

Another type of painting shows assemblages of gods and teachers designed to show the succession of authority in a particular sect or school. Such paintings occur again both as *thang-kas* and wall-paintings and, in context, indicate the tradition to which the monastery belonged. These paintings, generally designed as a tree, group together not only mortal teachers but also the guardian deities of a particular tradition, and they reflect the high importance accorded to the teacher in Lamaism; initiation into a specific ritual or practice with its power to effect liberation could be received only from a qualified teacher who had himself been consecrated. The disciplines and rites had to be taught by one endowed with appropriate authority and judgement as to the aptitudes of the aspirant and to be valid a tradition had to be traced through its practitioners back to India.

Yet another group of paintings revives an old Buddhist tradition, that of narrative, historical and legendary representation. Events from the life of the historical Buddha, a popular theme at the outset of Buddhist art and again later in countries of South-East Asia which adopted Buddhism and Indian culture, are represented on *thang-kas* in small scenes around the central figure of the Buddha. Similarly the lives of other figures, such as Tsong-kha-pa, were illustrated, sometimes spread over sets of paintings. There were also representations of historical figures who had attained particular distinction as teachers or mystics. As such they fulfilled someting of the role of the historical Buddha and were thus deified; in Tibetan tradition, moreover, they were also likely to be incarnations of specific deities or saints. A remarkable feature of such paintings – though by no means all – was the element of portraiture. Despite considerable formalisation many representations of princes of the church, translators, abbots and mystics seem to be based on observation and are sometimes rendered with power and expressiveness, though it is, of course, not possible to know how faithful any such apparent portraits may be. This apparent portraiture also appears in metal images (2).

A history of Tibetan painting cannot yet be written and only some general observations will be offered here. Native traditions recognise the existence of different schools and of external influences operating in Tibetan art. It is probable that the earliest influences on Tibetan painting came from Kashmir, eastern India and Nepal at the time of the Second Diffusion (from the end of the tenth century) to be followed by that of China. Direct Buddhist

57 Cloth-painting of the Buddha, seated and making the earth-touching gesture symbolising the Enlightenment. His garment is divided into the prescribed patches of the monk's robe and around him are scenes from former existences. 28 × 19 in. Reign-mark of the Wanli emperor (AD 1573–1619).

Indian influence cannot long have survived the destruction of Buddhism in eastern India and its gradual disappearance from Kashmir, complete by the end of the fourteenth century. Eastern Indian tendencies were, however, allied to Nepalese art which continued to exert an influence for many centuries. The early painting of western Tibet exhibits a Kashmiri character for geographical and historical reasons which have been explained elsewhere; its colour schemes and line differ from those of Nepal though Nepalese influence gradually becomes apparent. Western Tibetan painting becomes increasingly provincialised despite the appearance of Islamic features from the west. By the seventeenth century western Tibet would have become increasingly subject to the artistic domination of styles favoured in Lhasa. The importance of the Nepalese manner was paramount in south Tibet where Gyantse was an important centre, though the presence of Chinese elements dates from the close contacts between the Mongols in China and the Sa-skya-pa rulers and there is literary reference to Chinese artists. Nepalese painting with its predilection for red and the compartmentalisation of the field (pl. 2) remained a strong influence. Ngor, an influential centre founded in 1429, was decorated by Newar painters. Chinese influence seems integrated into a Tibetan tradition by the seventeenth century as may be seen in the British Museum's painting (57) executed during the reign of the Wanli emperor (1573–1619). This painting marks the acceptance of landscape after the Chinese manner. A sense of space becomes pervasive and this formula, though it stiffens and becomes highly stylised and seems often entirely ornamental, is characteristic. From the eighteenth century, with the assertion of Chinese political power over Tibet, there is always strong Chinese influence but it remains blended with developed elements from the earlier period with its mixed and varied traditions.

IMAGES IN METAL

The small metal statuary of Tibet is as well known abroad as the scroll-painting. The subjects represented are predominantly Buddhist, although the developed Bon-po also produced metal images very similar to the Buddhist (15). In this religious art-form the Tibetans followed a long tradition set by their Indian masters, who produced metal sculpture in increasing quantities, if one may judge from the style of surviving examples, from about the middle of the first millennium AD. The excavations at Nalanda, the great monastic university so influential throughout the Buddhist world from at least the seventh century, yielded no less than five hundred bronzes and elsewhere in eastern India from about the seventh century Buddhist metal sculpture is associated with monastic sites. Buddhist metal sculpture was also produced in Kashmir, the other remaining stronghold of Buddhism in India before its extinction. In China Buddhism created its own tradition of metal sculpture in the early first millennium AD which began with imitations of Indian models, but it soon acquired a quite distinctive Chinese character. A closer dependence on Indian models was retained by the metal statuary of Nepal, Burma and Java. In Nepal the conservatism which prolonged the life of Indian statuary styles long after they had disappeared from their country of origin exercised a profound influence on Tibet which depended greatly on Nepalese inspiration and craftsmen until modern times.

It is hardly surprising that there are so many metal images abroad, for their quantity in Tibet must have been enormous. Commissioning and worshipping images produced merit, as did offerings to monasteries where images were housed; altars in assembly-halls, cells, private chapels, houses and tents might hold more than one image and this was particularly the case in the many monasteries. Images were commissioned for various ceremonies and to ward off evil influences and certain deities were thought capable of procuring specific benefits.

Metal images are often called bronzes but that term, strictly applicable only to a copper and tin alloy, should in this context be considered conventional: copper alloy would, without previous analysis, be a safer designation for base metal statuary. In Tibetan statuary the metals are, indeed, most commonly copper alloys but bronze rarely, if ever, occurs; copper containing low levels of trace elements is not uncommon but brass predominates. These statements summarise a number of recent investigations including an extensive sampling of Nepalese, Tibetan and Sino-Tibetan bronzes in the British Museum (Oddy and Zwalf *Aspects of Tibetan Metallurgy*, 1981). The results also support tentative conclusions that relatively high zinc percentages are more characteristic, at an early period, of

58 Gilt figure of Mahakala, one of the great protectors, holding a chopper, drum, skull-garland, a broken trident, noose and skull cup with an elephant skin stretched behind him. Garlanded with heads, he stands on the elephant-headed Ganesa. Height 8¼ in. 18th century AD.

western Tibetan alloys; the percentage of zinc is higher in pieces presumed recent as might already have been expected for technical reasons connected with the difficulties of smelting zinc, while high copper alloys may testify to the presence in Tibet of Newar craftsmen from Nepal where copper statuary has long been traditional particularly because copper gives a better surface for fire-gilding. There is now more experimental evidence also that small quantities of gold were mixed with the alloys as a form of offering. The Tibetans themselves possessed a literary classification of metals and alloys used for statuary but the terms are for the most part obscure and for further discussion of this problem the interested reader is referred to the publication already mentioned.

Metal statuary was produced in a number of ways. A method common throughout the ancient world is casting by the lost wax method (cire perdue). By this method images were sculpted in wax over an earthen or mud core or from a solid piece of wax; the wax was then covered in mud, usually in thin successive layers which were carefully allowed to dry. This covering formed the mould in which there were openings to allow the wax to run out when heated and its metal replacement to be poured in. The mould was then broken and the metal figure tooled where necessary to achieve a better finish. Depending on whether the original sculpture had been modelled over a core or completely in wax the casting was hollow or solid; in Tibet at least partly hollow casting was necessary for sacred fillings, charms, grains, semi-precious stones and talismans to be inserted. Lost wax casting is still practised in Nepal, where it was probably brought from India, and is traditional among certain classes of Newar craftsmen. As there is abundant evidence that Newar artists worked in Tibet from an early period it may be assumed that their methods, which have come to differ slightly from the Indian, were also used by them in Tibet and adopted by their Tibetan imitators. These Newar techniques may well go back to a considerable antiquity and the same may be true of their application in Tibet. A distinctive feature of Newar wax casting is the production of the image from separate parts which are fitted together after casting. This method was uncommon in India where the image was usually modelled and cast in one piece. (For an eye-witness account of modern Newar casting and relevant discussions, see Lo Bue in Oddy and Zwalf, 1981.)

Another casting method is said to have the advantage that the mould is not destroyed every time and this is claimed in a recent publication to have been a commoner technique in Tibet than that just described. By this method an object is encased in a mud-pack which is then carefully sliced at the sides to produce two half moulds. In a variant of this method the mould is produced in already separate halves each covered with charcoal powder which makes possible their separation without slicing. With this method openings (sprues) are, of course, also provided for the introduction of the molten metal and care is taken that the moulds are properly dried to prevent their cracking. When an image is to be made the halves are joined. There are, however, technical reasons for disbelieving the claim for such widespread use since sand or mud-pack casting can be successfully used only on objects without difficult projections (undercutting) and the examination of Tibetan images does not support the claim. Yet another method of making metal images was to use hammered and worked sheets of various sizes. The process is of cold working throughout (28). The different parts were worked to the required shapes by the use of moulds supported on a kind of wooden anvil round which the metal was hammered; they were then, if required, engraved, chased, or incised along lines previously marked out; by using the repoussé technique, or embossing, shapes were pushed out from the back of the surface to be decorated.

Whether cast or made by cold working, separate parts had to be joined. This was done by riveting, soldering, the use of tenons and dovetailing castellated edges. The very common lotus base of images and back-plates or mandorlas were joined by slotting the upper part into the lower. Slots were also used to attach sets of multiple arms to images of complicated iconography. Small separate attributes were fixed into holes as pins or held between curved fingers and are thus easily lost.

Tibetan images were also, but not always, gilt, either by amalgam gilding, i.e., the application of hot liquid gold mixed with mercury onto a surface which has already been rubbed down and covered with a layer of mercury, or cold gilding, which is an application of gold paint or thin gold leaf; to apply gold leaf a burnishing tool has to be used. Laboratory studies of amalgam gilding by the British Museum and an eye-witness account of its present mode of application in Nepal have been published in Oddy and Zwalf (1981).

Two further decorative devices inherited from India were used on Tibetan images as well as on ritual and secular objects. Stones of turquoise and coral, coloured glass and paste, held in small cloisons, enhanced the image and drew attention to the ornaments; the stones were often set into necklaces, pendants, bracelets and crowns or were used to indicate the so-called third eye. This use of stones, particularly turquoise, is especially characteristic of the Nepalese taste but is found also in Sino-Tibetan bronzes. The use of metal inlays contrasting with the colour of the principal alloy is another characteristic decorative device. Silver and copper inlays are used to emphasise ornaments and facial features: the eye, the central mark on the forehead as well as necklaces, pendants, chains and floral motifs in textiles may be inlaid with silver; copper inlay is also used to vary the appearance of an image's dress as well as to pick out lips. Inlay has probably been less frequent in more recent pieces.

Heads are frequently found painted: on peaceful deities the hair is blue and the face painted in gold: the painting of important images with 'face-gold' is reported to have been an annual custom; fierce deities are apt to have red paint in the hair. Pigments occur on other parts of the figure with evidently decorative intention, such as red on lips and inside the mouth. The red has been identified in some cases as red lead and cinnabar and the blue as azurite.

There is a Tibetan classification of metal statuary which divides it by origin into two main groups and at the same time appears to take note of stylistic differences. The first group is of foreign images, though they were presumably known in Tibet: Indian, Mongolian (Hor), Nepalese and Chinese; the second is Tibetan. It is difficult to evaluate these divisions: there is certainly no regular correspondence between the sometimes quite detailed descriptions and types of statuary known today. It must be assumed that the types of Indian bronzes listed are Buddhist; and, unless they are imitations, it would follow that they are earlier than the disappearance of Buddhism in India. The description of eastern Indian bronzes, in particular

59 Manjusri, Bodhisattva of Wisdom, with raised sword and book. Brass inlaid with silver, copper and green stone. Height 5½ in. Eastern India or south Tibet, 12th century AD.

those of Bengal, seems consistent with what is known of their style before its disappearance. It has, indeed, recently seemed possible to some scholars to assign certain bronzes of a strongly eastern Indian type to Tibet but it can as well be argued that they were imports or the work of immigrant craftsmen (59). Their excellent state of preservation – understandable if they had been kept in the favourable conditions of the Tibetan climate and the monasteries – distinguishes them from excavated Indian material, which is naturally more corroded, and the difference should perhaps be treated with some caution. But other descriptions and categories in the Indian classification are more puzzling. Of the other foreign bronzes, a Mongolian group seems to include bronzes from the time of Godan, Kublai Khan's father, and his successors. Another 'Mongolian' group may refer to earlier work from Xinjiang, which was an influential source of Buddhist art in Central Asia in the first millennium AD: a Khotanese artist is reported to have come to Tibet in the eighth century. The similarity claimed between the 'middle' Nepalese and eastern Indian groups is, with some caution, acceptable. Chinese bronzes are divided into old and new, the old being perhaps of the Tang period (618–907) while the new are explicitly ascribed to the Yongle emperor (1403–24) in whose reign a quantity of Lamaistic bronzes were manufactured in China (54). Tibetan bronzes are said to begin with the reign of the first Buddhist monarch (Srong-brtsan-sgam-po, 627–650) but nothing can be confidently claimed for that period and the rest of the First Diffusion (627–838) although the description of the ninth-century bronzes as very similar to Indian work and inlaid with silver and copper carries a certain conviction. This was the age of the great expansion of Buddhist bronze casting in eastern India and Kashmir. Indian craftsmen are, moreover, claimed as their authors.

Another category of Tibetan metal images is associated with the bKa'-gdams-pa sect. It thus belongs to the Buddhist revival, or Second Diffusion, particularly as continued by the Tibetan activity (1042–54) of Atisa, the Indian scholar and virtual founder of that sect. Centres of production in south Tibet are named and most of the work is likened to ninth-century statuary though stated, unlike the earlier group, not to be of high enough standard of craftsmanship to be compared with Indian images. The verdict is hard to interpret but may refer to an early Tibetan style regarded as inferior because it was provincial. Only some bronzes are claimed as being almost indistinguishable in style and quality from Indian images. These are amongst the work done for Ye-shes-'od and his great-nephew Byang-chub-'od, the eleventh-century monk-kings of Gu-ge in western Tibet. There may be a reference here to the creation of images in the Kashmir style following the return of Tibetan scholars from Kashmir accompanied by craftsmen.

Large bronzes are said to have been made by the bKa'-rgyud-pa sect at the same time, built up in parts and reaching a storey or more in height.

Another school, named after the artist Sle'u chung-pa, seems to be Sino-Tibetan in the Yongle tradition. The same style is said to have been followed in the best images cast in Lhasa, but it is not clear whether this is a reference to the 'Dod-li images, named after a workshop situated at the foot of the Potala in Lhasa and founded in the time of the fifth Dalai Lama (1617–82). This appears to have become the official workshop of the Tibetan government with a vast output into modern times. Another centre was at the seat of the Panchen Lama at Tashilhunpo. It is said to have produced work in the 'Dod-li style of Lhasa. Sir Charles Bell visited what he called the metal factory at Tashilhunpo and found 'only thirty artisans at work turning out five hundred images of the god, Tse-pa-me ... for distribution to various monasteries throughout Tibet'. We may be dealing here with references to a Tibetan national style. Derge in eastern Tibet was famous for its metalwork and, in addition to decorated wares, is also credited with the making of images in recent times, reportedly in a Chinese style.

IMAGES IN CLAY AND STUCCO

Images were made from both stucco and clay. They could be very large and are reported from several major shrines. Most of a three-dimensional *mandala* in stucco existed until recently in a western Tibetan temple and elsewhere in western Tibet, including Ladakh, stucco modelling in the round or in high relief has been recorded. Stucco or lime-plaster is a medium widely used in the classical eastern Mediterranean, from where it may have spread during the early centuries of the Christian era into Iran, Pakistan and Afghanistan. It was used abundantly for Buddhist sculpture in the late Gandhara period (fourth – fifth centuries AD) and in Buddhist Central Asia, until its absorption into the Muslim world around the beginning of the second millennium AD. On the borders of China Proper large Buddhist images in the Dunhuang caves were made of stucco and, as in other regions of stucco statuary, painted and gilt. Dunhuang was, before 848, under Tibetan occupation for some time but the impulsion to model in stucco is more likely to have entered Tibet from other areas of Buddhist artistic influence, such as the Tarim Basin of Xinjiang to the north, Kashmir in the west and Bihar in the south.

A published description of clay modelling states that the hollow figure was built up from below with clay of fine and even consistency made into a thin hard wall with the help of paper. The construction of larger clay images was a lengthy process performed in sections, with a charcoal fire placed in the interior to help dry the fabric while the outer surface was covered with a wet cloth to prevent cracking and to facilitate the join with the next stage of construction. A number of no doubt recent smaller clay figures in the British Museum seem to depend for their stability on a heavy surface application of lacquer and the internal use of straw to bind the clay.

Stamped images and miniature *stupas* in clay, called *tsha-tsha*, were exceedingly common. The *tsha-tshas* were normally round or oval plaques, sometimes with a flat base and a pointed arch at the top, and the image and its surrounding features in relief. They were made in great numbers in Buddhist India and have survived particularly from Bodh Gaya – the historical Buddha's place of Enlightenment – where they were doubtless manufactured as pilgrims' souvenirs. Very similar stamped plaques were also common in Burma, Thailand and Java at the time that Buddhism was entering Tibet and it is surprising that no eastern Indian examples have been reported or collected from the country. The stamped *stupa* in the round was also known in India. Most *tsha-tshas* were small and showed the principal figure (60), sometimes with attendants or architectural features, but larger *tsha-tshas* laid out more like a *thang-ka* with the principal deity surrounded by an entourage were also known. Both plaques and *stupas* were often

60 (left) Painted *tsha-tsha* or impressed clay plaque showing a seated Yogin with a meditation band. Height 4½ in. 18th century AD (?).

61 (right) Round amulet box (*gahu*), with a silver filigree band and glass window showing a circular painted *tsha-tsha* inside with the Buddha holding his bowl and flanked by bodhisattvas. Diameter 2⅜ in. 19th–20th century AD.

inscribed. Numerous figures from the pantheon were represented: Tathagatas, bodhisattvas, goddesses, special tutelaries, ancient teachers and ascetics, reformers and Dalai Lamas. Early *tsha-tshas* from western Tibet were plain and stamped out of white chalky clay; later *tsha-tshas* were often painted. While some may have been baked they usually appear to have been sun-dried, or hardened by being mixed with soaked and beaten paper pulp.

Tsha-tshas could contain sanctifying substances: they were mixed with the ashes and pulverised bones of lamas or incarnations and one *tsha-tsha* in the British Museum showing the seventh Dalai Lama (1708–57) is said to contain his remains. Such *tsha-tshas* were highly prized as talismans. Making *tsha-thas* was considered a means of acquiring merit and they were produced in enormous quantities and put to many uses, being distributed and sold by monasteries as pilgrims' charms, placed on altars and carried inside charm boxes which often had windows through which they were visible (61); they were put by devotees into *stupas* or special shrines in the middle of wide roads or at crossroads and the tops of passes; when the shrines were full they were closed up. They were also placed in makeshift roadside shelters or under ledges and used as sacred fillings of images along with other objects. A wooden portable shrine in the British Museum is full of embedded *tsha-tshas* of various deities (62).

62 Interior of portable wooden shrine set with *tsha-tshas* and painted with offerings on the inner faces of the doors. The central *tsha-tsha* shows the Yellow Church tutelary Vajrabhairava below an enshrined Buddha and surrounded by various deities and lamas. Height 16¼ in. 19th century AD.

63 Oval stone carved in low relief Tibetan characters with the six-syllable *mantra*, or spell, of Avalokitesvara (*Om mani-padme hum*), in the form of an invocation to his female partner, Tara, whom it represents as the god's wisdom-partner. Length 7 in., height 5 in.

STONE CARVING

Stone seems to have been barely used for statuary. A number of large images carved into rock faces are known; smaller shallow relief carving occurs far more often. Figures of deities and teachers, shrines, animals and sacred formulas were cut in low relief on separate stone surfaces or onto rock faces. The separate carvings served as votive offerings placed at dangerous or auspicious places, tops of passes, bridges, narrow roads, hilltops and crossroads. Continuous low relief carving on rock faces could also be found at such places or along pilgrimage circuits and such carving was commonly painted in bright colours. The best known type of low relief carving in stone is the six-syllable *mantra* carved either in Tibetan script or a variety of ancient Indian ornamental character used in Tibet (63). Such stones were placed as offerings and were also made into walls dividing a road along its length for some distance between shrines: the whole stretch was worshipped by the rite of circumambulation. Since the six-syllable formula is the special *mantra* of

Avalokitesvara, low relief carving of that Bodhisattva might be found with it. The formula was also carved on rock faces, one line above the other and each letter painted a specific colour so that such rock-faces presented 'vertical stripes of brilliant colours'.

Carving in the round or high relief figures, the stone equivalents of the huge production of statuary in metal and, to a lesser extent, in papier-mâché, clay and stucco, is almost unknown. A carving against a back-plate in Indian and Nepalese fashion of great technical accomplishment in the British Museum at present stands alone (64).

64 Mahakala, as protector of the tent, standing on a human figure and with a mace across his arms, holding a chopper and skull cap. The 'parent' Buddha in his head-dress is Akshobhya. The back-plate shows gods and animals. Schist. Height 7½ in. 17th century AD.

An interesting stone object from Tibet also in the British Museum casts some light on Tibetan religious attitudes. It is a damaged replica of the Mahabodhi Temple, one of the few pre-Muslim structures to have survived in eastern India which, though much restored, in its present form goes back substantially to the Gupta period (AD 320–550) and incorporates even older elements. It is here that the historical Buddha is said to have experienced Enlightenment beneath the sacred fig tree whose supposed descendant grows beside the temple. A replica of the Mahabodhi Temple with subsidiary structures and a delimiting wall was known to be preserved at the monastery of sNar-thang just before the Second World War and republished in a Chinese publication of 1957. Tibetan pilgrimages to the Mahabodhi site seem never to have ceased even after the end of Buddhism in India and the temple is at present a focus for large numbers of Tibetan exiles. The Museum's replica may have been produced in India as a pilgrimage memento some thousand years ago or it could be a later Tibetan imitation (65).

65 Schist model of the Mahabodhi temple at Bodh Gaya, India, the place of the Buddha's Enlightenment. Perhaps from a miniature reproduction of the whole site in a Tibetan monastery. Height 4¼ in. Indian work (13th century AD?) or later Tibetan copy(?).

66 Seated and painted wooden Buddha wearing the traditional patched robe richly decorated with wide floral border. Height 9 in. Perhaps eastern Tibet or China, 18th–19th century AD.

WOOD CARVINGS

Wood is far less uncommon in Tibet than is sometimes supposed, though large parts of the country are above the tree-line and transport between the central valleys and the wooded regions, mainly in the south-east, along the Himalayan slopes and below the northern uplands, is not easy. Nevertheless, wood was used widely in building for beams, pillars, doorways and furniture, and some remarkable early architectural carving has been described and photographed. Wooden images are, however, not commonly reported or found in foreign collections and it is perhaps significant that one wooden seated Buddha in the British Museum is in a style reminiscent of Nepalese work and may be from Gyantse on the trade-route from the south, while another figure of the Buddha may come from the Sino-Tibetan borderlands, where wood is again more easily obtainable (66). Articles of

67a Oblong wooden printing block carved in reverse in the 'head-possessing' Tibetan character. 12½ × 4¼ in. 19th century AD (?).

religious use are, nevertheless, frequently found in wood; these include portable altars, ritual daggers (*phur-bu*) for protection against hostile spirits, the often very beautifully carved wooden book-covers (oblong planks preserving the format of the Indian palm-leaf strip though they enclosed paper sheets; pl. 1) and wood-blocks for printing. These wood-blocks, a Chinese invention, were used to print the text of the sacred books, the two collections of which number 108 and 225 volumes respectively, and also served to produce in vast numbers the paper charms placed inside prayer-wheels and images, and flags bearing lucky devices and auspicious formulas attached to sticks or cord. Charms used as flags were also printed on cloth and *thang-kas* could be produced from outlines printed with wood-blocks. The shape of these blocks varied according to their intended use. For books and many charms they retained the horizontal oblong shape (67a, b) of the manuscript page which derived from the format of the smaller palm-leaf strip on which Indian and Nepalese texts were written from ancient times almost to the present day. Blocks for flags and pictures were square or oblong, but higher than they were wide. The wood-blocks were always carved mirror-style. It is not known how long this form of printing has been used in Tibet; its introduction may well be earlier than the invention of printing from moveable types in Europe (around 1439). The earliest dated blockprint is a Chinese Buddhist text (AD 868) found at Dunhuang on the western borders of China, which, with other parts of Central Asia, had recently been under Tibetan rule. But the technique is certainly a Chinese invention and there is no evidence of its use in Tibet at so early a date. The complete Tibetan canon was not printed from wood-blocks in Tibet until 1731 at sNar-thang: a later edition was printed at Derge from metal plates but the use of metal to make plates for printing is exceptional. Blockprinting in Tibet may go back to the eleventh century,

120

67b Modern impression from the printing block (left) with spells (*mantras*) of Manjusri, Avalokitesvara, Vajrapani, the Dhyani Buddha of Long Life, Amitayus, and Hayagriva.

when the Chinese already knew moveable type, which was never adopted in Tibet.

In the preparation of a wood-block a piece of suitable wood, which may be hazel, birch or walnut, was cut to the required shape. The page or sheet to be printed, if not otherwise available, was copied or removed from an existing book and pasted, written face downwards, onto the surface to be cut, thus transferring the ink of the original to the uncut block. The paper was then removed by scraping or rubbing, or left on the wood with some oil added to make the letters or outline stand out. The block was carved with a suitable engraving tool so that the letters or figures stood out in sufficient relief. While this was done the wood was moistened to make the cutting easier. This task required considerable time and skill for text blocks might be carved on both faces. Once the block had been cut it was repeatedly oiled to strengthen the wood and make easier the removal of pages during printing.

Printing was done by groups of two or three monks, dividing the operations between them: putting the block on a bench, rubbing ink over it with a pad, cutting and laying the paper on the block, running a roller or brush over it. At Derge the finished sheets were taken to another part of the printing shop to be sorted and checked. According to sect the edges of the sheets were sometimes marked in red (for the old orders) or yellow (for the reformed and dominant Yellow Church).

At the great monasteries like sNar-thang, Derge, sKu-'bum in Amdo and Choni in Gansu, complete editions of the scriptures were obtainable and large rooms housed tens of thousands of blocks on numbered shelves, but almost every monastery had its printing shop which produced at least charms and flags. A book was usually ordered afresh, rather than bought from a previous owner; the purchaser often had to supply the ink and paper, and the monks were paid for the work. If the monastery with the required blocks was distant the costs of the work and those of transport might be greater than the expense of having a text copied from an existing book nearer to hand. In either case, of course, merit was acquired by printers, copyists and the persons commissioning the work. The paper was said to come from the inner bark of a laurel shrub (*Daphne cannabina*) or from roots and bamboo and to have been made in Tibet as well as imported in considerable quantity from China and Bhutan.

CHARM BOXES

A very common popular religious object was the portable charm or amulet case (*gahu*), consisting of red leather or cloth packets or wooden and metal boxes. Those found in foreign collections are usually made of metal, some with openings to show an image and some without; their contents include printed or written charms, objects blessed by a lama, fragments of a monk's robe, relics, and images. Images of Tara were very common, for she was thought to work quickly against misfortune and disease. Women in particular wore them on necklaces but both sexes carried them, particularly for protection on a journey, suspending them for greater efficacy, both front and back, on straps that passed over one shoulder and under the opposite arm. Sometimes they were hung from the belt or attached to the saddlebag. Otherwise they were kept on the household altar or they could be set up as independent shrines on a rock or raised piece of ground, where they were worshipped with prostrations and the ancient and orthodox rite of clockwise circumambulation.

The *gahus* were sometimes made of more than one metal: copper alloy for the sides and back, the front being of silver, often elaborately worked with

68 Talisman box (*gahu*). Its brass top is decorated with an openwork pattern against a contrasting copper background. 4 × 3 × 1⅜ in. 19th century AD.

69 Ladies at Shigatse wearing ear-pendants, necklaces, 'horned' head-dresses and other ornaments. (Photo H. E. Richardson)

embossed scrolling and other designs, human and animal figures and Buddhist sacred symbols, while the edges of the cover and the window were bordered by pearled wire (61). The decoration was often also in filigree scroll and leaf designs interspersed with turquoise, coral and paste. The central design might also be a sacred monogram. The shapes were various: round, rectangular and oval or shrine-shaped with ogival tops, an outline often repeated by the window which in recent times was closed with imported glass. For attachment they might have tubes of baluster form or lugs at the sides (68). The windowless type of *gahu* was sometimes unusually large. At the New Year Festival members of the nobility, dressed in clothes said to have been worn by the early kings, suspended from their necks great circular *gahus* covered in concentric rows of turquoise but very large studded *gahus* could also be found amongst persons of humbler station; the aristocratic 'beer-girls' who served refreshment at the same festival wore more than one in the form of a square with triangular projections on each side, a shape also not confined to wealthier women. But a noblewoman's *gahu* could be of gold set with diamonds, rubies, sapphires and turquoises. The windowless *gahus* seem indeed to have become more like ornaments and small examples were worn as part of the male head-dress as a sign of rank.

123

5
Food, Dress and Jewellery

The material life of Tibet offered great contrasts, not less striking than in the religious sphere, where mastery of complex and subtle theologies existed alongside the belief that spirits with the power to affect human affairs lurked and threatened at very turn. At the beginning of this century Tibet would readily have been thought backward by the European observer. Wheeled vehicles were not used and armour, made both of mail and lamellae, or small metal strips threaded by leather thongs, was worn not only by the contingents traditionally furnished by nobles and high-ranking officials at the New Year tournaments but also by cavalry and infantry when it met the Younghusband Mission in 1903–4. On that occasion even horses were still clothed in armour. Armour was heavy (70) but the average Tibetan was hardy and set little store by personal comfort yet where prestige was involved he could be uninhibited in expenditure on ornament and display, and his deep attachment to religion and the advantages it might bring were expressed by considerable outlay on the highly embellished cult objects and talismans used personally or offered to the temples. Domestic furniture was usually of the simplest except in the private chapel; ordinary national dress was functional and unpretentious but a 'best' garment might be of the finest imported material. Ecclesiastical and secular clothing showed the greatest variety and splendour: wealthier or higher clergy might wear garments far removed from the apostolic simplicity of Buddhist ideals (pl. 3), religious dancers and oracles wore the finest silks (pl. 7) and noblemen and officials had formal dress which was distinguished by its costliness and the variations employed to express rank. The use of jewellery was common to both sexes and the dress of women expressed a profound concern with fashion and an almost overloaded display of ornament. The splendour of textiles, the use of precious metals, inlaying with precious and semi-precious stones (71), variations in baser alloys to produce differences in tone on the same object, appliqué designs in a variety of materials and the use of paint all contributed to an exuberance of colour. Accentuated by the clear air of the plateau, it

125

70 Steel helmet of long curved overlapping strips meeting at the top under a holder for a lost plume and edged with a series of small plates secured, like the longer strips, with leather thongs. Height 14 in. 19th century AD or earlier (?).

71 Silver buckle, perhaps for a shirt. The centrepiece, with raised decoration, is set with coral and turquoise; at both sides is a butterfly motif. Length 3 in. Perhaps from eastern Tibet, 19th century AD.

made an official occasion, tournaments, festivals and processions memorably impressive. Colour films and photographs of such events in the old Lhasa survive and the impression they leave is of a world like that of the late mediaeval miniature brought back to life with its display and luxury at the apex of a society, sophisticated and ordered but with a limited technology and no doubt a poverty often cheerfully borne and perhaps also not as extreme as elsewhere.

126

EATING AND DRINKING

The general diet, to which reference has already been made, was, if adequate, limited and monotonous. The *haute cuisine* of the better-off tended towards the Chinese and was eaten with chopsticks where the poorer classes used a spoon. The Tibetan most commonly ate *rtsam-pa* or barley flour, mixed with tea, butter and cheese and kneaded into little balls in a wooden bowl (72) which he carried in a fold of his gown; the same bowl was used for tea, which was always Chinese, though of various kinds, and imported in the form of bricks. The leaves and twigs were broken off and boiled in a cauldron with water and soda and then poured through a strainer into a churn where it was mixed with butter and salt. It was then ready for the tea-pot. When it was poured out the butter was apt to form a scum which was blown aside and put into a grease pot; poorer people reused it for the next preparation of tea. The usual tea-pot was of earthenware but for special occasions there were tea-pots of metal, such as copper, with gold and silver mounts and decorative spouts and handles made with a dragon motif (pl. 5). The average con-

72 Wooden bowl for tea and mixing *rtsam-pa*. Greatest diameter 4¾ in. Early 20th century AD.

73 Low wooden table with folding front and sides and open at the back. It is decorated with dragons, flowers and scrolling and painted in gold, red and green. Height 10¼ in., length at top 22½ in. 19th–20th century AD.

128

sumption of tea, a highly nourishing combination in the severe Tibetan climate, was put by one observer as high as forty to fifty cupfuls a day with some drinking perhaps as few as twenty and others as many as eighty. The wooden bowls when empty were licked clean before being put away. In better society the tea-cup was of china or even jade mounted on a stand, and covered with a lid which might be of silver and gilt and worked to various designs (pl. 9).

For drinking tea and eating the Tibetans had characteristic low tables, which were used in religious as well as secular contexts (73). They consisted of a flat top, three hinged sides and one open length facing the user. The hinged sides fold into the top, short lengths first, making the tables easily transportable, an appropriate feature in a society with a significant nomad population and a taste for picnics and other open-air occasions. Such tables were made of wood and metal; the sides often afforded an opportunity for exuberant open-work decoration with dragon's heads and vegetal motifs. An example in the British Museum painted in green, red and gold illustrates the Tibetan love for the bold use of colours.

Beer, made from barley mixed with yeast and left to ferment for a number of days, was another widespread drink. It was drunk by workers in the fields, at picnics and entertainments and served at the colourful New Year ceremonies by young women dressed in all their finery. It was also used for religious offerings to the fierce deities. Various jugs were used: large spouted and globular pitchers with handles made of hammered copper and brass such as were also used for water and tea; other designs included a form with a circular body and flat sides like a canteen on a foot and mounted with decorated handle and spout. Such flasks were inlaid with copper, gold and silver or partly gilt at Chamdo in eastern Tibet, a region famous for its metalwork. Another type of water and beer-jug was cylindrical and decorated with embossed work or inlaid, also in the manner of eastern Tibet.

The Tibetans carried about with them eating sets consisting of sheaths holding knives, spoons, small forks and chopsticks. The sheaths were made of wood with ornamental metal mounts or covered with animal skin and suspended from the belt. Chopsticks were more widespread in eastern Tibet on, or within, the borders of China Proper, and the knife reminds us that, despite the Buddhist prohibition on taking life, meat – especially yak's meat and mutton – was an integral part of Tibetan diet, being available where vegetables were not and an almost inevitable concession to geography and climate.

DRESS

Tibetan dress presented great contrasts and variety. The basic national garment was the *chu-pa,* a long-sleeved and loose cloak, worn by men and women and fastened around the waist by a belt or sash. Since it is very wide it overlaps on the wearer's left and passes diagonally from the shoulder to below the right arm where it can billow out above the belt and be used as a large pocket in which a man may keep his food and tea bowl and other small necessaries (or even a dog) not habitually hung from the belt. The cut, colour and material of the *chu-pa* differed widely; it was worn shorter by countryfolk and nomads than by townspeople and women wore it longer than men. The nomads wore *chu-pas* of sheepskin with the wool inside; different grades of native cloth and deerskin were used and these were more durable than imported broadcloth, satin or silk. The more formal *chu-pas* were even buttoned where the poorer man found the puffed-out pocket convenient. *Chu-pas* could be trimmed with fur in winter, which for the official classes was fixed between a date in December and another in April. During this period lay and ecclesiastical officials had to wear fur hats and cloaks according to the rules governing the materials, colours and patterns they might wear for a given season. However cold it was outside this period furs might not be worn! The everyday *chu-pa* of native wool became almost waterproof with wear: it retained not only the original oil but was soon stained with the omnipresent butter of the Tibetan diet.

Among the sedentary folk and wealthier classes the *chu-pa* was worn with various additions such as shirts, trousers, waistcoats and jackets. Lhasa women wore a petticoat or apron with bright horizontal stripes of different colours over a long sleeveless dress and a long-sleeved blouse. Head-dresses varied by region; they were often made of wooden or cloth frames sewn with jewels, semi-precious stones and rings of shell (74). Rank and office as well as regional variation and season governed men's headgear. There were hats of many kinds, some inherited from the period of Mongolian rule and an incongruous note was struck in recent times by the popularity of a felt hat like the European Homburg imported from India.

Monks had three principal garments, in keeping with the ancient Buddhist code, but they differed from those formerly in use in India. They were usually red instead of saffron and, to take account of the climate, woollen instead of cotton. The Tibetan cleric wore a lower garment or skirt held up around his waist by a sash and gathered concertina-fashion at the front. An upper garment introduced, it is said, by the reformer Tsong-kha-pa, was a sleeveless waistcoat, made partly of brocaded silk in the case of wealthier monks or higher clergy (pl. 3). Its ends were tucked into the lower garment and it was sometimes replaced or supplemented by a similar but long-

74 Male and female servants of a noble family in ceremonial dress, the men wearing the official's ear-ring of their master and the women high head-dresses. (Photo H. E. Richardson)

sleeved jacket. Over it was worn a voluminous shawl running across the body over the left shoulder and under the right arm. This was considered the equivalent of the ancient Indian upper garment. The third traditional garment, an overgarment, was worn for certain ceremonies over all the previously described garments but could also be worn beneath the shawl. It was yellow and thus represented a return to the Indian monastic colour. Another garment was a heavy cape worn particularly during services when the monks sat often for very long periods in the cold temple assembly-hall. The twill woven example in the British Museum is of native wool and pleated. In front, from the sash, which was yellow if the wearer belonged to the dominant Yellow Church, hung the traditional water bottle, reduced

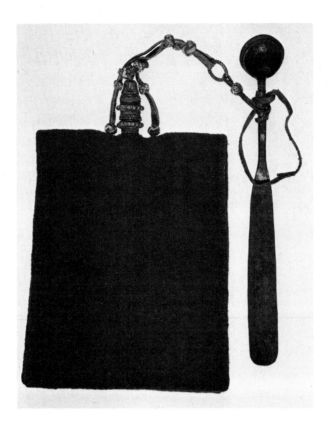

75 Monk's metal water bottle for rinsing his mouth, in a red woollen bag worn from the belt. The uncommon ladle with it may have been for holy water kept in the bottle for another purpose. Bag: 8½ × 7 in., length of ladle 11 in. 19th–20th century AD.

almost to a formality (75). From it the monk was supposed to rinse his mouth in the morning. It was a small metal vessel, entirely hidden in a larger, rectangular textile bag, which, as in the British Museum's example, could be of native woollen cloth, but brightly brocaded cases were also used. Those of the ruling Yellow Church were yellow. Two other pieces of traditional monastic equipment, also nearly reduced to a ceremonial value and represented in the British Museum, are the staff and begging bowl, said to have been carried on begging tours and used for alms-begging rites in monasteries. The staff, which was carried by travelling pilgrims also, is a long stick surmounted by an arrangement of four curved prongs meeting at the top. From each prong hung a number of rings and these, traditionally, made the monk's presence known on his begging rounds, for when he struck the staff on the ground the rings jingled, and the householder was reminded of his pious duty. The sound was also supposed to drown the noises of the outer world and to warn small creatures in case they were accidently crushed

132

76 Crested yellow woollen hat commonly worn by monks of the Yellow Church. Its introduction is attributed to dGe-'dun grub-pa (1391–1475). The height of the crest is said to rise according to educational qualification. Greatest height 28 in. 19th century AD.

underfoot by the monk. The bowl in the British Museum is made of brass and 'clothed' in a decorated textile of yellow cotton and patchwork brocades. Almost universal, however, was the rosary of 108 beads which was not carried by monks alone. Its use was widespread also among the laity both for the repetition of prayers and also for making ordinary calculations.

Further concessions to the Tibetan climate were the monk's use of boots and his wearing of trousers and *chu-pa* when travelling. Hats may be another Himalayan innovation, at least in their great variety, for tradition attributes to early evangelists the introduction of monastic headgear and a pointed hat appears on the small figure of a monk (?) worshipper on the base of a Bengali image of the goddess Tara now in the Dacca Museum and datable to the early second millennium AD. The pointed monk's hat in Tibet extends over the ears, usually in long lappets. According to sect such hats were red when worn by members of the older schools, or yellow with the dGe-lugs-pa or reformed followers of Tsong-kha-pa. They were reserved for special

77 Oracle's round metal breast plaque with a mystic syllable in the centre, representing the deity working through the oracle. On the gilt surround are embossed skeletons, scrolling and Buddhist cult objects. Diameter 8¼ in. 19th century AD.

ceremonies. A common monk's hat is of a yellow crested type which writers have compared with plumed helmets of classical antiquity (76). It was worn on many occasions and generally out of doors. Hats varied greatly according to rank, educational standing, sect and occasion. A few are represented in the British Museum's collection. A type of hat associated with the rNying-ma-pa can be seen on representations of Padmasambhava (22), another of the bKa'-rgyud-pa tradition on an embroidered *thang-ka* (56), and those curious to see a greater range may consult the line drawings in Waddell (1895) and Tucci (1980). An example of a hat used on special occasions is one made of lacquered papier-mâché and worn by recognised incarnations when riding out of doors (31).

A range of particularly splendid garments and hats was worn by clerical dancers, exorcists and oracles. Dancers had long, wide-sleeved silk gowns often sewn together out of various pieces of brocade (pl. 7) over which they wore the scalloped and decorated 'cloud collar', used also for other rituals as

78 Pair of oracle's boots covered in silk with leather soles also partly covered in silk. On the uppers are represented dragons' faces by appliqué patches and strips of satin and gold-threaded brocade. Height 14 in. 19th century AD.

well as on images, and aprons of embroidered or brocaded silk. Oracles, too, wore aprons and, like some dancers, a gilt bordered and silvered round plaque on their beasts with, in the middle, a mystic syllable in relief set with turquoise, coral, or entirely of metal (77). They also wore helmets or cloth hats stitched with a striking triple-eye motif above a tiara of five skulls; the same striking eye as part of a stylised dragon's face is stitched on a pair of boots in the British Museum said to be those of an oracle (78). Various ceremonies required tall black hats with the brim commonly bordered with black fur. Another type of special headgear consisted of a crown of five plaques, each of which represents one of the five Dhyani Buddhas. For some exorcistic ceremonies bone aprons were worn, consisting of short plaques of human bone carved with small figures and connected in a criss-cross pattern by strings of round beads also made of human bone. The workmanship on the British Museum's examples as on some reported elsewhere is Nepalese.

135

79 A group of noblewomen wearing jewellery including talisman boxes, long necklaces, seed pearls
and the characteristic forward-facing ear-pendants beneath their 'horned' head-dresses.
(Photo H. E. Richardson)

JEWELLERY

Tibetan men and women were greatly attached to personal adornment though it did not always have a purely ornamental function. Official dress, as already mentioned, could produce displays of intense colour and clerical garments were not always of a dull sobriety. The amulet cases carried by men and women varied in design and shape and gave an opportunity for the craftsmen to express the characteristically Tibetan love of colour and inlay, whether using semi-precious stones or imitations. The principal stones, coral and turquoise, were also found on images and many ritual articles. Coral was imported and the best turquoises came from Persia and China but there was also native turquoise. The taste for coral goes back to the thirteenth century, for Marco Polo (c. 1254–1324) writing of Tibet (or its north-eastern portion) says that the women 'wear it about their necks and with it ornament their idols'. Stones were also used on the various frames worn as a head-dress by women in central Tibet. Rising in a semi-circle or fixed like a crescent suggesting horns, they were made of wood or bamboo and cloth and carried corals, turquoise, pearls and amber. Such head-dresses were not confined to the rich, but those of poorer women had only a few stones of turquoise, coral and rings of shell. Elsewhere in Tibet the women plaited their hair into braids and these carried ornaments, lengths of material to which stones and silver discs with variously worked designs were attached. A notable Lhasa fashion among women was that of wearing ear pendants not from the ears themselves but hooked from the hair or head-dress just above, so that they faced the viewer (79). These pendants had a characteristic shape and consisted of several parts, each with a different outline – circular, leaf- and flower-shaped and set with turquoise on a silver or copper alloy mount. Women wore necklaces, sometimes of huge amber beads, charm boxes, strings of seed-pearls hanging from the left shoulder in a broad swathe to the end of which necklaces were attached and belts, such as the British Museum's example, of cruciform design made with silver links and ornamented with a panel of turquoises where the three lengths joined. The necklaces were sometimes long enough to reach to the bottom of the pendant of such a belt well below the waist. On their belts and sashes men and women wore chatelaines (80), or ornamental attachments of metal or metal on leather from which were hung various useful articles such as milk-pail hooks, tweezers, toothpicks, needlecases, flint and tinder pouches, sheaths for knives and chopsticks, pencases, inkbottles and stamps for personal seals (81).

Men wore far fewer ornaments. Apart from the amulet cases hung round their necks or from the shoulder strap when travelling, they had a number of different kinds of ear-ring whose weight was sometimes eased by a chain or

137

strip of material passing over the top of the ear. An ear-ring with hoop and pendant hung from one ear and a rough stone was attached to the other. Officials wore one of a prescribed kind from the left ear: long and narrow, with a pearl in the middle and turquoises above and below, except that the lower pointed end was required to be an imitation (8). Such pendants were also permitted to their servants. Above a certain grade an official had also to wear an amulet box in a top-knot of his hair and a similar box was worn by his servant in his pigtail.

Artefacts of Tibetan culture continue to be made in the southern borderlands outside political Tibet not only amongst the settled inhabitants but also and farther afield by refugee craftsmen. Without the directing patronage of a capital and great religious centres, however, the arts and crafts seem doomed to remain provincial and to lack development. The demand for such objects in political Tibet itself may revive with the reopening of places of worship and a more flexible attitude by the authorities to the traditional ways. A recent newspaper article described an old silversmith beating out a silver butter lamp as a private commission for a local monastery. It remains to be seen whether younger men will be trained in the traditional skills.

80 Silver and brass chatelaine with a turquoise set in a filigree surround attached to a loop with leaf decoration. Two lugs at the back are for attachment to a belt. Length 3 in. 19th century AD.

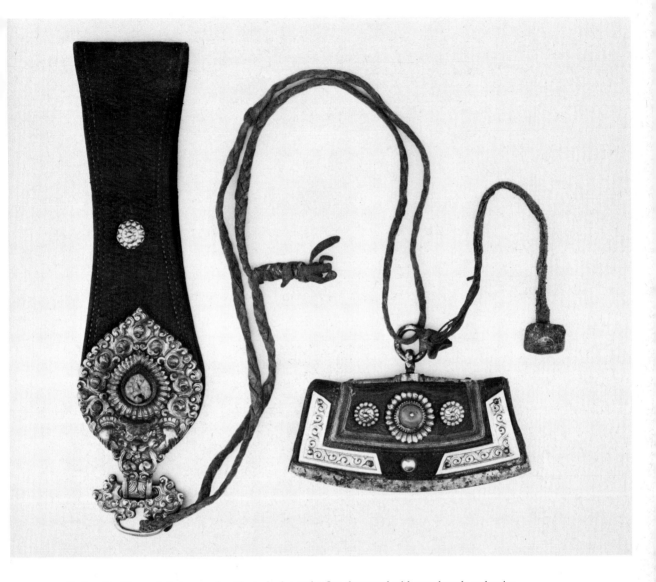

81 Leather flint and tinder pouch with steel edge and a flap decorated with metal studs and strips. In the centre is a coral bead in a floral setting. The pouch is attached to a leather suspension strap with a metal chatelaine. Width of pouch 5 in., length of strap 9¾ in. Perhaps from eastern Tibet. 19th century AD.

Select Bibliography

Béguin, G. *Dieux et démons de l'Himâlaya*, Paris, 1977.

Bell, Sir Charles *The people of Tibet*, Oxford, 1928.

Dagyab, L. S. *Tibetan religious art*, 2 vols, Wiesbaden, 1977.

Ekvall, R. B. *Religious observances in Tibet*, Chicago and London, 1964.

Getty, A. *The gods of northern Buddhism*, Oxford, 1928 (reprinted 1963).

Gordon, A. K. *The iconography of Tibetan Lamaism*, New York, 1939.

Gordon, A. K. *Tibetan religious art*, New York, 1952.

Govida, Li Gotami *Tibet in pictures*, 2 vols, Berkeley, 1979.

Harrer, H. *Seven years in Tibet*, London, 1953.

Hoffmann, H. *The religions of Tibet*, London, 1961.

Hoffmann, H. *Tibet, a handbook*, Bloomington, 1975.

Huntington, John C. *The phur-pa, Tibetan ritual daggers*, Ascona, 1965.

Karmay, H. *Early Sino-Tibetan art*, Warminster, 1975.

Lauf, D. I. *Tibetan sacred art*, Berkeley and London, 1976.

Lowry, J. *Tibetan art*, London, 1973.

Macgregor, J. *Tibet: a chronicle of exploration*, London, 1970.

Nebesky-Wojkowitz, R. de *Oracles and demons of Tibet*, London and The Hague, 1956.

Newark Museum *Catalogue of the Tibetan collection*, 5 vols, Newark, 1950–71.

Norbu, T. J. and C. Turnbull *Tibet, its history religion and people*, Harmondsworth, 1969 (New York 1968, London 1969).

Oddy, W. A. and W. Zwalf *Aspects of Tibetan metallurgy*, London, 1981. (British Museum Occasional Papers, no. 15.)

Olschak, B. C. and G. T. Wangyal *Mystic art of ancient Tibet*, London, 1973.

Pal, P. *The art of Tibet*, New York, 1969.

Pott, P. H. *Introduction to the Tibetan collection of the National Museum of Ethnology, Leiden*, Leiden, 1951.

Richardson, H. E. *Tibet and its history*, London, 1962.

Rockhill, W. W. *Notes on the ethnology of Tibet*, Washington, 1895.

Shakabpa, W. D. *Tibet, a political history*, New Haven and London, 1967.

Sierksma, F. *Tibet's terrifying deities*, The Hague and Paris, 1966.

Singh, Madanjeet *Himalayan art*, London and Melbourne, 1968.

Snellgrove, D. L. *Buddhist Himalaya*, Oxford, 1957.

Snellgrove, D. L. *Himalayan pilgrimage*, Oxford, 1961.

Snellgrove, D. L. *Nine ways of Bon*, London, 1967.

Snellgrove, D. L. *The Hevajra Tantra*, 2 vols, Oxford, 1959.

Snellgrove, D. L. and H. E. Richardson *A cultural history of Tibet*, London, 1968 (reprinted Boulder, Colorado 1980).

Snellgrove, D. L. and T. Skorupski *The cultural heritage of Ladakh*, 2 vols, Warminster, 1977–80.

Stein, R. A. *Tibetan civilization*, London, 1972.

Tucci, G. *The ancient civilisation of Transhimalaya*, London, 1973.

Tucci, G. *The religions of Tibet*, London and Henley, 1980.

Tucci, G. *The theory and practice of the mandala*, London, 1969.

Tucci, G. *Tibetan painted scrolls*, 3 vols, Rome, 1949.

Tucci, G. *Tibet, land of snows*, London, 1967.

Tung, R. J. *A portrait of lost Tibet*, London, 1980.

Waddell, L. A. *The Buddhism of Tibet or Lamaism*, London, 1895.

Index

Words and names transliterated from Tibetan are listed according to their radical letters.

Figures in italics refer to the black and white illustrations, those in bold type to the colour.

142

143

Index